More BBQ and GRILLING

FOR THE BIG GREEN EGG® & OTHER KAMADO-STYLE COOKERS

AN INDEPENDENT COOKBOOK INCLUDING NEW SMOKING, GRILLING, BAKING AND ROASTING RECIPES

ERIC C. MITCHELL

PITMASTER OF THE COMPETITION BARBECUE TEAM YABBA DABBA QUE! AND CERTIFIED JUDGE BY THE KANSAS CITY BARBEQUE SOCIETY

PHOTOGRAPHY BY KEN GOODMAN

PAGE STREET
PUBLISHING CO.

PAGE STREET
PUBLISHING CO.

First published in 2016 by
Page Street Publishing Co.
27 Congress Street, Suite 103
Salem, MA 01970
www.pagestreetpublishing.com

Distributed by Macmillan; sales in Canada by The Canadian Manda Group.

19 18 17 16 1 2 3 4 5

ISBN13:9781624142376

ISBN10:1624142370

Library of Congress Control Number: 2015952108

Cover and book design by Page Street Publishing Co.

Photography by Ken Goodman

Printed and bound in the U.S.A.

Page Street is proud to be a member of 1% for the Planet. Members donate one percent of their sales to one or more of the over 1,500 environmental and sustainability charities across the globe who participate in this program.

★ DEDICATION ★

To my wife, Cindi; my children, Greg and Rebecca;
and to all my family—whether by blood, marriage or smoke.

INTRODUCTION

Cooking outdoors is more than good food. Many gatherings of family and friends include a barbecue or cookout. It's a very social event, surrounded by great food, in the warm sun, with lots of stories and goofing around. The kids can also have free range and have their own adventures. A catered event is good, but being able to provide an afternoon or evening of homestyle, backyard comfort food will inspire you to express your passion for cooking on the Egg and all the good times and memories that come with it.

When I was finishing up my first cookbook, *Smoke It Like a Pro*, I curiously determined that I had another cookbook in me. I was passionate about creating and sharing recipes and techniques about cooking on the Big Green Egg and other Kamado cookers. This second book continues well beyond the first book and details more recipes for the Big Green Egg that are adventurous and fun to make. These recipes take eggheads to new places with new flavors they may not have dared try before. None of these are hard to make, and they will add different techniques and approaches to your repertoire of delicious dishes on the Egg. Consider it this way: most Big Green Egg owners got started because they wanted to do more than grill burgers and dogs on a gas grill. Now that you know how to cook on the Egg and are well accustomed to its versatility, why not kick it up a notch or two? I trust this book will help you do just that. Even if you are new to the Egg, you will learn fast.

The Big Green Egg and I have been keeping each other company since the year 2000.

I am not a chef or a cook but rather a "food enthusiast." I grew up with a large family of one brother, four sisters and 38 first cousins. Everyone in my family is a great cook. Several were farmers, and I grew up on farm-raised meats, fruits and vegetables. Every gathering centers on family and food.

In 2006, after seeing barbecue competition shows on TV, I asked Cindi if she would consider entering competition barbecue contests. We first became certified Kansas City Barbecue Society (KCBS) judges. We judged a few contests and decided we could cook just as well as the competitors. We also became members of the New England Barbecue Society (NEBS). After winning our first $5 plastic trophy, we were hooked! In 2007, we were awarded the New England Barbecue Society's (NEBS) Rookie Team of the Year!

We have won many awards and have competed twice at the Jack Daniels' World Championship Invitational Barbecue in Lynchburg, Tennessee, and once at the American Royal Invitational in Kansas City, Missouri.

In addition to competing, for the last several years we have also been performing food demonstrations at Big Green Egg dealerships in New England and New York for Tarantin Industries, the Big Green Egg distributor. We demonstrate the versatility of the Egg with all we cook.

This second book is set up differently than my first book, *Smoke It Like a Pro*. This book has chapters for certain kinds of food, meats, vegetables, baking, casseroles and desserts. The first book had separate chapters showing the style of cooking, such as grilling, smoking and deep-frying, and the cooking technique for each. Chapter 10 of this book includes much of the same information and techniques and understanding how the Egg works.

I am confident that this book will further your passion for cooking on the Big Green Egg and cooking outdoors for friends and family. I believe that when Eggheads go to restaurants and order something different or special, that they intuitively wonder, "How can I cook this on the Egg?" With this cookbook, you'll learn new techniques, tricks and recipes to fulfill your Egg-loving dreams.

CHAPTER 1

BODACIOUS BEEF & LUSCIOUS LAMB

When it comes to beef and lamb, there are so many different cuts that are well suited for barbecue or grilling. Steaks, roasts, kabobs, burgers and meatballs are all outdoor favorites. Beef is very prevalent in the United States and South America, but it is widely available all over the world, including Asia, the Mediterranean and the Middle East. Lamb is very popular in the Mediterranean and the Middle East but is now widely available and cooked worldwide. The same cut of beef is cooked differently depending on the region it comes from. Steak and hamburger do great all by themselves when grilled with just salt and pepper to medium rare. Choice or higher grading is best. While some people can eat a good, simple steak meal after meal, I prefer to mix it up with different marinade flavorings, spices and even stuffing. This attention will also allow you to enjoy lesser grade beef. You can create different flavors, and they are all delicious.

Grilling beef and lamb over a charcoal fire is the best way and, to many, the only way to serve it. Whether it's a sear for fast cooks or a bark for slow cooks, the smoke flavor produced by this method is without comparison.

RIB EYE TOMAHAWKS WITH HORSERADISH SAUCE

Tomahawk steaks are bone-in rib eye steaks with the bones "frenched." They are known for their tender, juicy and beefy qualities. These steaks are great cooked with just salt and pepper. Cooked this simple way, the juicy beef flavor will stand out. The horseradish sauce provides a contrasting flavor, which complements the steak. This method of searing is adapted from T Rex's method. T Rex is a frequent contributor to the Big Green Egg forum.

MAKES ABOUT 4 SERVINGS

4 rib eye steaks, 1½-inch (4-cm) thick, choice or higher

1 tbsp (18 g) kosher salt

2 tsp (10 g) black pepper, coarse ground

2 tbsp (30 ml) olive oil

4 tbsp (57 g) unsalted butter

HORSERADISH SAUCE

1 cup (236 ml) sour cream

6 tbsp (90 g) prepared horseradish, drained

2 tsp (10 ml) Dijon mustard

¼ cup (10 g) finely chopped chives or green onions

¼ tsp kosher salt

¼ tsp freshly ground black pepper

Set the Egg for 700°F (371°C) direct. With the top and bottom vents wide open, light the fire and close the Egg. When the Egg gets up to about 250°F (121°C) dome, about 10 minutes, close the bottom screen. When the Egg approaches 700°F (371°C) dome, about 15 to 20 minutes, leave the top of the daisy wheel open.

While the Egg is heating up, cut any outside fat from the edges of the steaks and "french" the bones down to the meat by cutting and scraping the meat down to form a "hook." Rub with olive oil and sprinkle with salt and pepper and rub into the steaks. Let the steaks come up to room temperature, about 15 minutes.

Prepare the horseradish sauce by combining all of the ingredients in a small bowl, then refrigerate until ready to serve.

When the Egg is up to 700°F (371°C), burp the Egg and be careful for flash back (see page 208). Place the steaks on the oiled cast-iron grate. With the dome open, sear for 1½ minutes, then twist the steak and turn 90 degrees for another minute. Flip the steaks and sear the same as the first side. When complete, remove the steaks from the Egg and set to rest for 20 minutes. Meanwhile, set the Egg for 400°F (200°C) indirect by adding the plate setter and shutting the vents to lower the temperature. When 20 minutes have passed, place the steaks back on the Egg, indirect, and roast 4 minutes per side for medium rare. After the last flip, place a slice of unsalted butter on top of each steak to melt. Remove from the Egg, tent with aluminum foil and let rest for 10 minutes before serving. Serve with the horseradish sauce on the side.

CARIBBEAN STRIP STEAK WITH ONION AND RUM GLAZE

New York strip steak is known by other names, such as shell, Delmonico or Kansas City strip. It is known for its tender, juicy and beefy qualities. These steaks are great cooked with just salt and pepper. This method of searing is adapted from T Rex's method. It provides a seared steak with a juicy and tender inside. The onion rum sauce will take you on a little vacation!

MAKES ABOUT 4 SERVINGS

4 New York strip steaks, 1½-inch (4-cm) thick, choice or higher

Olive oil, for the steaks

Salt and pepper, for the steaks

2 tbsp (30 g) unsalted butter

2 medium onions

2 tsp (6 g) garlic, minced

¼ tsp kosher salt

¼ tsp black pepper, freshly ground

1 cup (240 ml) dark rum

½ cup (120 ml) low-sodium beef stock

2 tbsp (30 ml) molasses

4 tbsp (60 g) unsalted butter, softened

Set the Egg for 700°F (371°C) direct. With the top and bottom vents wide open, light the fire and close the Egg. When the Egg gets up to about 250°F (121°C) dome, about 10 minutes, close the bottom screen. When the Egg approaches 700°F (371°C) dome, about 15 to 20 minutes, slide the top of the daisy wheel partially closed, leaving it three-quarters of the way open. Cut any outside fat from the edges of the steaks and rub them with olive oil. Sprinkle with salt and pepper and let the steaks come up to room temperature, about 15 minutes.

In a medium saucepan, melt the butter. Peel the onions and slice them into quarters, from stem to root. Add the sliced onions to the butter and sauté until the onions start to caramelize, about 10 minutes. Add the garlic, salt and pepper and stir for another 3 minutes. Add the rum and simmer for 10 more minutes, until the rum is reduced by half. Add the beef stock and molasses and stir. Simmer until slightly thickened, about 5 more minutes. When the Egg is up to 700°F (371°C), burp the Egg and place the steaks on the oiled cast-iron grate. Sear for 1½ minutes, and then turn the steaks 90 degrees for another minute. Flip the steaks and sear the same as the first side. When complete, remove the steaks from the Egg and set to rest for 20 minutes. Meanwhile, set the Egg for 400°F (200°C) indirect by adding the plate setter and shutting the vents to lower the temperature.

When 20 minutes have passed, place the steaks back on the Egg, indirect, and roast 4 minutes per side for medium rare. After the last flip, place 1 tablespoon (15 g) of unsalted butter on top of each steak to melt. Remove from the Egg, tent with aluminum foil and let rest for 10 minutes before saucing.

BEEF WELLINGTON

Beef tenderloin is the most tender part of the cow. It is very lean and should be cooked to no more than medium rare. Wellington is a trumped-up way to add flavor to the delicate roast while varying its texture. You can purchase a whole tenderloin, 6 to 8 pounds (2.7 to 3.6 kg), but I know the butchers at the big food clubs will cut a smaller piece for you. The prices are reasonable as well.

MAKES ABOUT 3 TO 4 SERVINGS

1 (2½ lb [1 kg]) center cut beef tenderloin, trimmed

2 tbsp (30 ml) olive oil

1 tbsp (6 g) kosher salt

½ tbsp (3 g) freshly ground black pepper

3 tbsp (45 ml) unsalted butter, softened

1 minced shallot

½ cup (120 g) mushrooms, minced

1 tbsp (1.6 g) dried thyme

1 tbsp (15 ml) red wine

1 sheet puff pastry from 17.5 oz (490 g) package of frozen puff pastry, thawed

1 large egg yolk, beaten

Trim any silver skin from the tenderloin and let it come up to room temperature. Coat the tenderloin with olive oil, salt and pepper. Set up the Egg for a direct grill at 450°F (230°C). With the top and bottom vents wide open, light the fire and close the Egg. When the Egg gets up to about 250°F (121°C) dome, about 10 minutes, close the bottom screen. When the Egg approaches 450°F (230°C) dome, about 10 minutes, slide the top of the daisy wheel partially closed, leaving it halfway open. Once the Egg is up to temperature, sear the tenderloin on all sides until browned, about 10 minutes, and then remove from the Egg and let it cool on a wire rack.

While the tenderloin is resting, place the butter, shallot, mushrooms and thyme in a frying pan and cook on a 400°F (200°C) Egg until the shallots and mushrooms have softened, about 5 minutes. Reduce the temperature of the Egg from 450°F (230°C) to 400°F (200°C) by closing the daisy wheel, leaving a quarter of it open.

Add the wine and continue to cook for another 5 minutes, until the wine has reduced. Once cooked, remove from the Egg and let cool. On a flat surface, lay out the puff pastry sheet and place the cooked tenderloin in the center. Place the cooled shallot and mushroom mixture on top of the tenderloin, wrap it up in the pastry and seal the edges with egg wash. Coat the outside with the beaten egg.

Place the wrapped tenderloin in a roasting pan and roast on the Egg at 450°F (230°C) indirect for about 15 minutes or until the internal temperature reaches 125°F (52°C). Place the cooked Wellington on a cooling rack under foil for about 10 minutes, and then slice into 1½- to 2-inch (38- to 51-mm) slices and serve.

TEXAS BEEF SAUSAGE

Beef sausages in Central Texas are largely attributed to the German immigrants in the area in the 1800s. These sausages are primarily beef with a little pork added to bind them together. Many sausage makers in Texas will add curing agents to cold or hot smoked beef sausages. This recipe is for fresh sausage to be hot smoked on the Egg until fully cooked.

As an alternative, you can change the proportion of beef to pork or add additional spices, like garlic powder, cumin and coriander, to your taste. You can make up a patty prior to casing and fry it up to see if the flavors and texture suit you.

If you don't have a meat grinder, you can ask your butcher to grind it for you. If you don't have a sausage stuffer, you can make a fattie (see page 54), or grill the beef sausage as meatballs.

MAKES ABOUT 12 SERVINGS

2½ lb (1.1 kg) beef, round or chuck, sinew and gristle removed

½ lb (227 g) pork shoulder, bone removed

½ lb (227 g) beef fat

2 tbsp (36 g) kosher salt

2 tbsp (6 g) paprika

1 tbsp (3 g) black pepper

½ tsp cayenne pepper

Hog casings

Cut the beef, fat and pork shoulder into 1-inch by 1-inch (2.5-cm by 2.5-cm) strips, removing silver skin and cartilage. Using a coarse-grind plate, grind the meat a few pieces at a time, then grind a piece of fat. Alternate grinding several pieces of meat with a piece of fat to get a good mix.

In a large bowl, add the remainder of the ingredients, except the casings, and mix them gently by hand with half of the ground meat. You can tell that the spices are mixed in well by a uniform pattern in the bowl. Don't overhandle the meat or it will be less juicy when cooked. Add the remainder of the ground meat to the bowl and gently mix. Refrigerate the mix overnight before filling the casings.

Soak the casings for at least an hour. Fill the casings with a sausage stuffing attachment or your grinder and go slowly to prevent air pockets. The casings can be twisted to form links, about 8 inches (20 cm) long. Refrigerate the stuffed sausage until ready to cook.

Set the Egg for 250°F (121°C) indirect with a drip pan. With the top and bottom vents wide open, light the fire and close the Egg. When the Egg gets up to about 250°F (121°C) dome, about 10 minutes, close the bottom screen and slide the top of the daisy wheel closed, leaving the petals halfway open. Once the fire is well lit, add 3 chunks of hickory or white oak. Once the smoke has settled down to a bluish-gray color, place the sausage on the Egg and cook for 2 hours, until the internal temperature reaches 165°F (74°C). Remove from the heat, tent with foil and let rest for 5 minutes before serving.

RACK OF LAMB

Lamb is very popular in other parts of the world, but historically not so much in the United States. Nowadays, rack of lamb is available in most large supermarkets and wholesale clubs. It grills extremely well, giving a crispy outside and a tender, medium rare inside.

MAKES 6 TO 8 SERVINGS

DRY RUB

1 tsp kosher salt

¼ tsp freshly ground black pepper

¼ cup (60 ml) prepared brown mustard with seeds

2 tsp (6 g) fresh garlic, minced

2 tbsp (5 g) fresh oregano, chopped

1 tsp dried basil

1 tsp dried thyme

¾ cup (110 g) bread crumbs

2 racks of lamb, 8 bones each

2 tbsp (30 ml) olive oil

In a small bowl, mix all of the dry rub ingredients together and set aside. Trim any visible fat from the racks. One end may be thicker than the other, because it has a layer of fat, with a thin layer of meat beneath it and another layer of fat under the thin layer of meat. Remove both layers of fat and any silver skin. French the bone tips by cutting off any fat, meat or tissue. Rub the racks with olive oil, and then rub both sides of the meat with the dry rub.

Set the Egg for 350°F (180°C) indirect with a drip pan. With the top and bottom vents wide open, light the fire and close the Egg. When the Egg gets up to about 250°F (121°C) dome, about 10 minutes, close the bottom screen. When the Egg approaches 350°F (180°C) dome, about 10 minutes, slide the top of the daisy wheel partially closed, leaving it a quarter of the way open. When the Egg is up to temperature, place the lamb racks on the grid, bone side down. Cook for 25 to 30 minutes, until the internal temperature in the thickest part reaches 125°F (52°C) for medium rare, rotating the meat every 10 minutes. When cooked, remove from the Egg and tent on a rack under aluminum foil for 10 minutes. Slice between the bones and serve.

SANTA MARIA TRI TIP

The tri tip comes from the bottom sirloin and weighs 1½ to 2½ pounds (680 to 1134 g). It is very popular on the West Coast, but has caught on here in the East. The roast is small and should not be overcooked. It needs to be cut thinly, across the grain. With this simple rub, and cooked to medium rare, it is very juicy and flavorful. A few years ago at a grilling competition, one of the categories was tri tip. I had never heard of it, but I purchased a whole case and started to practice how to cook it. You can marinate it, and it will also hold up to a spicier rub. I cooked a lot of tri tip that spring and enjoyed it every time. You can serve this Santa Maria style with pico de gallo or any other salsa. It's where the beef's at!

MAKES ABOUT 4 TO 6 SERVINGS

1 (1½ to 2½ lb [680g to 1134 g]) tri tip roast

2 tbsp (30 ml) olive oil

1 tsp kosher salt

1 tsp ground black pepper

2 tsp (6 g) fresh garlic, minced

Remove any silver skin from the tri tip and rub it with olive oil. Rub the salt, pepper and garlic onto the meat. Cover with plastic wrap and let it sit in the refrigerator for several hours or overnight.

Set the Egg for high heat, 500°F (260°C) direct. With the top and bottom vents wide open, light the fire and close the Egg. When the Egg gets up to about 250°F (121°C) dome, about 10 minutes, close the bottom screen. When the Egg approaches 500°F (260°C) dome, about 10 minutes, slide the top of the daisy wheel partially closed, leaving it halfway open. Remove the tri tip from the refrigerator and unwrap, letting it come up to room temperature, about 15 minutes. When the Egg is up to temperature, burp the Egg and sear the tri tip for 3 to 4 minutes per side. Remove the meat and reduce the temperature of the Egg to 350°F to 375°F (180°C to 190°C) by closing the daisy wheel and leaving a quarter open. Return the meat to the Egg and continue cooking until the internal temperature reaches 135°F (57°C), turning twice for about 12 minutes. When finished, remove from the Egg, cover with aluminum foil and let rest for 10 to 15 minutes. The internal temperature should rise to 145°F (63°C) for medium rare. Cut into thin slices across the grain and serve.

GRILLED KOREAN BEEF SHORT RIBS

Short ribs are very flavorful, but because of all of the collagen, they need to be braised or barbecued for a long time. This recipe calls for the rib meat to be sliced into ¼-inch (6-mm) thickness, which lets the tenderizing marinade work faster and allows for fast, direct grilling. The ribs can be served on a plate or in lettuce wraps with green onions and toasted sesame seeds.

MAKES ABOUT 6 SERVINGS

3 lb (1.4 kg) beef short ribs, at least 1-inch (2.5-cm) thick

MARINADE

½ cup (120 ml) soy sauce

3 tsp (9 g) garlic, minced

1 tbsp (15 g) fresh ginger, minced

2 tbsp (30 ml) rice wine vinegar

¼ cup (45 g) light brown sugar

2 tbsp (30 ml) sesame seed oil

1 tsp freshly ground black pepper

The ribs can either be "English cut" or "flanken cut" bone-in short ribs. The goal is to cut the meat into ¼-inch (6-mm) slices. The English cut is a single bone short rib bone. It will be about 2 inches (5 cm) wide and 3 to 4 inches (7.5 to 10 cm) long. The meat will be 1½ to 2 inches (4 to 5 cm) high on the bone. The meat needs to be sliced partially through. Remove all the fat and sinew and cut lengthwise down next to the bone until about ¼ inch (6 mm) of meat remains. Do not cut through. Lay the rib down like a book. Switch directions and slice a ¼-inch (6-mm) slice from the next side, stopping ¼ inch (6 mm) from the edge of the meat and not all the way through. The meat will look like an accordion. Continue slicing until the remaining piece of meat is ¼ inch (6 mm) thick, 2 or 3 more times.

The flanken cut is 2 or 3 ribs connected together but cut with a meat saw, perpendicular to the bone in ¼-inch (6-mm) pieces. You can ask your butcher to cut these. With either style, it is important to have the finished rib meat to be ¼ inch (6 mm) thick.

Prepare the marinade by combining all ingredients except the ribs in a small bowl, mixing well. When mixed, place the marinade in a 1 gallon (4 L) resealable plastic freezer bag. Add the ribs to the bag and massage the marinade into the meat. Marinate for 2 to 4 hours in the refrigerator, turning and massaging every hour.

Set up the Egg for 450°F (230°C) direct. With the top and bottom vents wide open, light the fire and close the Egg. When the Egg gets up to about 250°F (121°C) dome, about 10 minutes, close the bottom screen. When the Egg approaches 450°F (230°C) dome, about 10 minutes, slide the top of the daisy wheel partially closed, leaving it halfway open. Take the ribs from the marinade and discard the marinade. When the Egg is up to temperature, sear the ribs for 3 minutes per side, until the internal temperature reaches 140°F (60°C). Remove from the Egg and tent with aluminum foil on a rack, resting the meat for 5 minutes before serving.

MATAMBRE, ARGENTINE STUFFED FLANK STEAK

Flank steak has a very pronounced flavor but is very tough. When cooked to medium rare and sliced thinly and diagonally across the grain, it is very tender. Don't overcook it. This South American version seasons the flattened flank steak and stuffs it with vegetables, hard-boiled eggs and cheese. But you can use a variety of stuffing ingredients.

MAKES ABOUT 6 SERVINGS

1½ to 2½ lb (680 to 1134 g) flank steak

2 tbsp (30 ml) olive oil, divided

1 tsp kosher salt, divided

½ tsp black pepper, divided

1 tbsp (9 g) garlic, minced

1 tsp dried cumin

1 tsp dried oregano

½ cup (10 g) baby spinach leaves

2 carrots, thinly sliced, ⅛-inch (3-mm) sticks

1 medium onion, thinly sliced, ⅛-inch (3-mm) and separated

3 hard-boiled eggs, sliced in half lengthwise

1 red bell pepper, thinly sliced, ⅛-inch (3-mm) sticks

½ cup (45 g) grated Parmesan cheese

Butcher's twine

Lay the steak on a cutting board with the grain going away from you. With a sharp knife, butterfly the steak by slicing it horizontally at one end. Continue to slice horizontally until you reach about a ½ inch (12 mm) from the other side. Open the steak like a book. Turn the sliced steak so that the grain runs left to right. Place plastic wrap on top of the open steak and pound it flatter, using a mallet. Pound it to a uniform thickness of about ¼ inch (6 mm). When finished, remove the plastic wrap and rub the flattened side of the steak with half of the olive oil. Sprinkle the steak with half of the salt and pepper and all of the garlic, cumin and oregano. Lay the baby spinach leaves in a layer over the spices, staying 1 inch (2.5 cm) inside all of the steak edges.

About 1 inch (2.5 cm) in from the side of the steak nearest you, lay several carrot slices, lengthwise left to right. Next to the carrots, working your way toward the center of the steak, add some onions left to right. Next, make a row of hard-boiled egg halves from left to right, and then make a row of red pepper sticks. Repeat the rows with the remaining carrots, onion and pepper slices. Sprinkle the Parmesan cheese over the vegetables. Starting at the edge closest to you, roll the steak tightly over the row of eggs and continue to roll the meat, like a jelly roll, until it is fully rolled. Try to keep the roll as uniformly thick as you can. Tightly tie the roll with butcher twine in circles, every 1 inch (2.5 cm) or so. Rub the outside of the steak roll with the remaining olive oil and sprinkle with the remaining salt and pepper. If you are not cooking the matambre immediately, wrap it in plastic wrap and refrigerate for up to 4 hours.

Set the Egg for 450°F (230°C) direct. With the top and bottom vents wide open, light the fire and close the Egg. When the Egg gets up to about 250°F (121°C) dome, about 10 minutes, close the bottom screen. When the Egg approaches 450°F (230°C) dome, about 10 minutes, slide the top of the daisy wheel partially closed, leaving it halfway open. Remove the matambre from the refrigerator, unwrap it and let it come up to room temperature for about 15 minutes. When the Egg is up to temperature, burp the Egg and sear the steak for 2 minutes per side. Remove the meat from the Egg and reduce the temperature of the Egg to 350°F (180°C) indirect with a drip pan. When the Egg is back down to temperature, place the meat back on the grate until the internal temperature reaches 130°F (54°C). Remove from the Egg and tent with aluminum foil on a rack, resting the meat for 15 minutes. Slice in ½-inch (12-mm) slices across the grain and serve.

KOREAN BULGOGI

This marinated beef is traditionally cooked on a very hot grill or griddle. This recipe uses a Himalayan salt rock for a cooking surface. I prefer the 2-inch (5-cm) thick Salt Rox®. It can come up to temperature along with the Egg. The Salt Rox can be used at high heat and is great for meat, vegetables and even cookies! I talked with Max Rosen, aka "Mad Max Beyond Eggdome" at Dizzyfest in Virginia this year, and he loves it. The meat cooks quickly and picks up a hint of salt. Plan on cooking a little bit more than you wish to serve. Somehow, all of the bulgogi doesn't make it to the serving platter!

MAKES ABOUT 4 SERVINGS

MARINADE

½ cup (120 ml) low-sodium soy sauce

2 tbsp (30 ml) toasted sesame oil

2 tbsp (25 g) granulated sugar

1 tbsp (15 g) fresh ginger, minced

2 tsp (6 g) fresh garlic, minced

¼ tsp freshly ground black pepper

3 green onions, finely chopped

1 tbsp (10 g) toasted sesame seeds

2 lb (900 g) top sirloin roast or sirloin steak

In a small bowl, mix all of the marinade ingredients together. Remove any fat from the meat and slice it against the grain into ⅛-inch (3-mm) slices. In a resealable plastic bag, add the marinade and sliced meat and refrigerate for 2 to 4 hours.

Set the Egg for 500°F (260°C) direct. With the top and bottom vents wide open, light the fire and close the Egg. When the Egg gets up to about 250°F (121°C) dome, set the 2-inch (5-cm) salt block on a raised rack so it is further up in the dome of the Egg. Let the salt block come up to temperature along with the Egg, about 10 minutes, and close the bottom screen. When the Egg approaches 500°F (260°C) dome, about 10 to 15 minutes, slide the top of the daisy wheel partially closed, leaving it halfway open. Remove the sliced beef from the marinade and discard the marinade.

When the Egg is up to 500° (260°C), place the bulgogi on the salt block. Sear for 1 minute per side. When complete, remove the beef from the Egg and cook another batch. When finished cooking, sprinkle the steak with sesame seeds and green onions and serve.

SPICED MEDITERRANEAN LAMB CHOPS

Lamb is commonly cooked throughout the Mediterranean. It holds up to a flavorful marinade of garlic, ginger, herbs and spices. Cooked to medium rare, it is very tender and tasty.

MAKES ABOUT 6 SERVINGS

MARINADE

1 tsp sweet paprika

1 tsp chili powder

1 tsp ground cumin

1 tsp kosher salt

½ tsp freshly ground black pepper

1 tbsp (9 g) garlic, chopped

½ tbsp (8 g) fresh ginger, chopped

½ cup (120 ml) olive oil

⅓ cup (13 g) fresh cilantro, chopped

⅓ cup (13 g) fresh mint, chopped

½ cup (20 g) flat-leaf parsley, chopped

6 to 8 loin lamb chops

2 tbsp (30 ml) olive oil

In a medium bowl, combine all of the spices, garlic and ginger and mix well. Add the olive oil and mix, and then add the fresh herbs and mix. Place the chops and the marinade in a resealable plastic bag, refrigerate, and marinate for 1 to 3 hours, massaging occasionally.

Set the Egg for high heat, 450°F (230°C) direct. With the top and bottom vents wide open, light the fire and close the Egg. When the Egg gets up to about 250°F (121°C) dome, about 10 minutes, close the bottom screen. When the Egg approaches 450°F (230°C) dome, 10 to 15 minutes, slide the top of the daisy wheel partially closed, leaving it halfway open. Take the chops from the marinade and discard the marinade. Season the chops with salt and pepper and sear for 2 to 3 minutes per side. When the internal temperature reaches 125°F (52°C), remove from the Egg, cover with foil and let rest for 10 minutes before serving.

MOROCCAN BONELESS LEG OF LAMB

The combination of garlic, paprika, lemon juice, cumin and mint makes this a distinctive Moroccan marinade for the lamb. The marinade will stand well with the tender flavor of the lamb and is subtly spicy and aromatic.

MAKES ABOUT 8 SERVINGS

MARINADE

3 tbsp (45 ml) olive oil

2 tbsp (30 g) fresh garlic, minced

1 tbsp (6 g) sweet paprika

1 tbsp (15 ml) lemon juice

2 tsp (12 g) kosher salt

2 tsp (4 g) cumin

1 tsp freshly ground black pepper

¼ cup (10 g) fresh mint, chopped

¼ cup (10 g) fresh oregano, chopped

3 to 4 lb (1.4 to 1.8 kg) fresh boneless leg of lamb

1 tbsp (15 ml) olive oil

½ tsp freshly ground black pepper

1 tsp kosher salt

Butcher's twine

In a medium bowl, mix all of the marinade ingredients together except the mint and oregano. Once the ingredients are well blended, add the mint and oregano and mix well. Refrigerate the marinade until ready to put on the meat.

Prepare the boneless leg of lamb by laying it flat on a cutting board with the deboned side up. Remove any sinew or large pieces of fat. Place a piece of plastic wrap over the meat and pound with a mallet to even out the surface. Remove the plastic wrap and rub the marinade into the deboned side of the meat. Roll the meat into a tight roll and tie every 1 inch (2.5 cm) with butcher twine. Rub the outside of the roll with 1 tablespoon (15 ml) of olive oil and sprinkle with 1 teaspoon kosher salt and ½ teaspoon black pepper. Wrap the roll in plastic wrap and refrigerate for at least 4 hours or overnight.

Remove the roll from the refrigerator and unwrap about 30 minutes before cooking it to bring it up to room temperature.

Set the Egg for 350°F (180°C) indirect with a drip pan. With the top and bottom vents wide open, light the fire and close the Egg. When the Egg gets up to about 250°F (121°C) dome, about 10 minutes, close the bottom screen. When the Egg approaches 350°F (180°C) dome, about 10 minutes, slide the top of the daisy wheel partially closed, leaving it a quarter of the way open.

When the Egg is up to temperature, roast the lamb for 10 minutes per side, until the internal temperature reaches 130°F (54°C), about 30 to 40 minutes. Remove from the Egg and tent with aluminum foil on a rack, resting the meat for 10 minutes. Slice thinly, diagonally across the grain, and serve.

SZECHUAN BEEF STIR-FRY

Stir-frying is not very difficult; you just need to have all of your ingredients prepared and ready to use. The first time might seem hectic, but with very little practice, you will be stir-frying, bing, bang, boom! In this recipe, coating the beef in cornstarch is called velveting. It keeps the meat moist as it cooks until tender. You will taste the beef with the sweet, savory and salty sauce coating and a little heat from the chilies, and the carrots are delicious served al dente. With very little practice, you'll become a wok master.

MAKES ABOUT 6 SERVINGS

1 lb (450 g) flank steak or top round steak

4 tbsp (60 ml) vegetable oil

2 tsp (6 g) garlic, chopped

2 tsp (10 g) ginger, chopped

6 red chili peppers, stemmed, with the blossom end snipped off

1½ cups (225 g) carrots, sliced into matchsticks 2 inches (5cm) long

½ tsp kosher salt

½ tsp freshly ground black pepper

Sliced green onions

MARINADE

2 tbsp (30 ml) low-sodium soy sauce

2 tbsp (30 ml) rice wine vinegar

1 tbsp (12 g) light brown sugar

1 tsp cornstarch

¼ cup (360 ml) low-sodium chicken broth

Slice the beef into 2-inch (5-cm) long and ¼-inch (6-mm) thick slices, against the grain. In a medium bowl, mix the soy sauce, rice wine vinegar, brown sugar and the cornstarch, and add the sliced beef to coat.

Set the Egg for 450°F (230°C) dome, direct. With the top and bottom vents wide open, light the fire and close the Egg. When the Egg gets up to about 250°F (121°C) dome, about 10 minutes, close the bottom screen. When the Egg approaches 450°F (230°C) dome, about 10 to 15 minutes, slide the top of the daisy wheel partially closed, keeping it half open. When the dome thermometer reads 450° (230°C), place the wok on the grate that sits on the fire ring, keeping the dome open. Add 2 tablespoons (30 ml) oil and heat until a drop of water dances for one or two seconds on the side of the wok before evaporating. Add the garlic and ginger and stir-fry for about 30 seconds before removing from the wok. Add the chili peppers and stir-fry before removing from the wok.

Add 2 tablespoons (30 ml) oil and reheat the wok. Add the beef in one layer and stir-fry for 3 minutes, reserving the marinade. Add the sliced carrots and continue to stir-fry for another minute. Add the chicken broth mixture, the reserved marinade, the peppers, oil, garlic, ginger and salt and pepper back to the wok and continue to stir-fry until the sauce thickens and the carrots start to wilt, another 1 or 2 minutes. Remove all, add sliced green onion and serve.

PULLED BARBECUE BEEF

Pulled barbecue beef is similar in style to pulled pork, but the tastes are obviously different. By cooking at a low temperature for a long time, the beef comes off of the Egg moist, a little spicy and very beefy tasting. You can use a rump or a round roast from the rear of the steer, but the chuck is from the front shoulder and is more moist and flavorful. The pulled beef can be served on a plate, in a taco or even on a pizza! I prefer to eat it on a plain hamburger bun with fried onions on top. You can add additional barbecue sauce if you like. Pulled barbecue beef is worth the wait!

MAKES ABOUT 10 TO 12 SERVINGS

4 lb (1.8 kg) boneless chuck roast

2 tbsp (30 ml) olive oil

1 cup (120 g) beef rub

½ cup (125 ml) dark beer

2 tbsp (30 ml) Worcestershire sauce

1 large onion, diced

Trim any visible sinew or silver skin from the roast. After trimming the roast, add a coating of olive oil to all exposed meat, and then generously rub the roast with the beef rub. It can be wrapped and refrigerated for several hours after adding rub, until ready to barbecue.

Set the Egg for 250°F (130°C) indirect with a drip pan, with the charcoal filled to the top of the firebox. This is where it meets the fire ring. With the top and bottom vents wide open, light the fire and close the Egg. When the Egg gets up to about 250°F (121°C) dome, about 10 minutes, close the bottom screen and slide the top of the daisy wheel closed, leaving the petals halfway open. Prior to adding the meat, put in 2 chunks of white oak and 2 chunks of pecan. Initially, there will be very white, billowing smoke. This is bad, bitter smoke! Wait until the smoke has settled down to a softer, bluish-gray color, and add the roast to the grate. Cook at 250°F (130°C) until the internal temperature reaches 160°F (71°C), about 3 hours. Remove from the Egg and place the roast in a roasting pan or a disposable half pan. Add the beer, Worcestershire sauce and onion to the pan. Cover the pan with aluminum foil and return the roast to the Egg. Continue to cook at 250° (130°C) indirect for 1½ to 2 hours, until the internal temperature reaches 200°F (93°C). You can probe through the foil to check the temperature. At 200°F (93°C) internal, remove from the Egg. Place the pan in an empty cooler to rest and keep warm for about 1 hour. Remove the roast to a cutting board and remove the onion pieces from the juices. Start to pull the beef apart with 2 forks to shred. Cut away any gristle or white fat and discard it. Place the shredded beef back in the pan juices and toss. Serve warm.

GREG'S MOXIE-MARINATED STEAK TIPS

In my first book, Sully contributed his "top secret" recipe. My son Greg insists his version is "the one." They both taste great, so who am I to question? The preferred meat is flap meat from the bottom sirloin. When marinated, the meat will have a great char from the sugars in the soda, a tender inside flavored by the marinade, and a pink medium rare inside. The soda Greg prefers is Moxie®, but cola will do in a pinch. Moxie® and steak tips are not often heard of outside New England, but if you grill these over high heat and don't cook past medium rare, you'll show you can have both great tips and Moxie® wherever you are!

MAKES ABOUT 6 TO 8 SERVINGS

12 oz (350 ml) chili sauce

12 oz (350 ml) regular Moxie®, not diet

1 cup (240 ml) Italian salad dressing

1 cup (240 ml) cranberry juice

2 tbsp (23 g) brown sugar

4 lb (1.8 kg) flap steak

Mix all marinade ingredients in a bowl. Trim any visible fat or silver skin from the flap meat and cut into strips, about 6 to 8 inches (15 to 20 cm) long, along the grain. Place the strips in a resealable freezer bag. Pour the marinade over the meat and seal the bag. Rub the marinade around to ensure all the meat gets covered. Place in refrigerator for at least 8 hours, or up to 48 hours. Turn and flip the bag over every so often to ensure all the meat stays covered in the marinade.

Set the Egg for 450°F (230°C) dome direct. With the top and bottom vents wide open, light the fire and close the Egg. When the Egg gets up to about 250°F (121°C) dome, about 10 minutes, close the bottom screen. When the Egg approaches 450°F (230°C) dome, about 10 to 15 minutes, slide the top of the daisy wheel partially closed, leaving it halfway open. Grill the beef to about 140°F (60°C) internal, turning every 2 minutes for a total of 10 minutes. Let your steak tips rest for 10 minutes before slicing against the grain in 1/3-inch (8-mm) slices.

CHAPTER 2

FROM TAIL TO SNOUT, IT'S WHAT PORK'S ABOUT!

Pork is my favorite. The spectrum goes from juicy butt and shoulder to leaner pork chops and loins, and don't forget the ribs and bacon!

The cuts, like pork butt and ribs, are greatly benefited by longer cooking times at lower temperatures. The leaner pork chops and loins, I believe, require a brine to keep them juicy because they have so little fat. The pork today is raised to be much leaner than it was thirty years ago, but as the saying goes, "Where there's fat, there's flavor." Heritage breeds of pigs are more readily available and have more of the pork flavor that I grew up with.

The recipes in this chapter barbecue or grill many different ways. The flavors depend on the region, local customs and available ingredients. Pork can be slow cooked, brined, stuffed, smoked or grilled. It's all good. After all, it's pork!

PERNIL, PUERTO RICAN PORK SHOULDER, PICNIC CUT

Pernil is a traditional holiday roast in Puerto Rico. The picnic is good for this recipe because it is not lean and it has a skin on the top side. The skin, when crisped, makes cueritos, a crispy treat. There is really no need to wait for Christmas for this juicy, crispy and garlicky pork favorite!

MAKES ABOUT 12 SERVINGS

1 picnic cut from shoulder, 7–8 lb (3.2–3.6 kg)

1 tbsp (18 g) kosher salt

1 tbsp (2 g) dried oregano

2 tsp (4.5 g) freshly ground black pepper

4 tbsp (60 ml) olive oil

¼ cup (60 g) garlic, minced

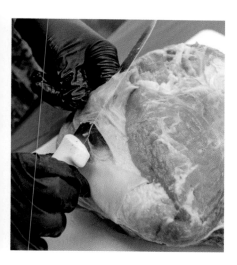

Wash the picnic and pat dry. Combine the dry ingredients in a food processor or grind with a mortar and pestle until pieces are well ground. Add 2 tablespoons (30 ml) of olive oil and all of the garlic to form a paste.

On the skin side (top) of the picnic, cut holes into the skin and into the meat about ½ inch (12 mm) deep and 2 inches (5 cm) apart. Push the paste into each hole, and then rub the paste on any exposed sides of the picnic. Refrigerate for 8 to 24 hours before cooking. Let the picnic come up to room temperature before cooking, about 1 hour.

Set the Egg for 325°F (160°C), indirect with a drip pan. With the top and bottom vents wide open, light the fire and close the Egg. When the Egg gets up to about 250°F (121°C) dome, about 10 minutes, close the bottom screen. When the Egg approaches 325°F (160°C) dome, about 10 minutes, slide the top of the daisy wheel partially closed, leaving it a quarter of the way open. Oil and salt the skin side and place the picnic, skin side up, over the drip pan. Cook for 4 to 5 hours, oiling the skin of the picnic on top every 30 minutes, until the internal temperature is about 190°F (88°C). The skin should be crisping up.

Once cooked, remove from the Egg and separate the skin from the picnic. Let the picnic rest, tented in foil, for about 30 minutes. If the skin is not crispy, return it to the Egg at about 400°F (200°C) for about 10 minutes. The skin will crisp up more as it cools.

Cut the skin into 1-inch (2.5-cm) squares and serve over the sliced or chopped picnic.

COMPETITION PORK RIBS, MEMPHIS DRY STYLE

I love pork ribs. I used to eat them wherever I could get them—at buffets, chain restaurants, mom-and-pop restaurants and even in the Caribbean at roadside "lolos." The ribs there were grilled, but really satisfied my cravings. Most ribs served at chains and buffets are steamed or boiled to get them tender, then grilled to crisp them up. I never knew how much flavor I was missing until I cooked them on the Egg. I have become a rib snob and no longer eat ribs that haven't come off a Big Green Egg!

For the Kansas City Barbecue Society (KCBS), the pork rib category can include pork spare ribs, St. Louis cut spare ribs or baby back ribs. I prefer to turn in St. Louis ribs. This cut is spare ribs trimmed so that the rack is rectangular in shape. One end will be as wide as the longest bone, about 6 inches (15 cm), and the other end where the shorter bones are will have some of the meat without bones in it. On the bone side of the slab, the thin meat flap that is near the knuckle of the shorter bones will be removed. Baby back ribs are cut up higher, closer to the back bone, and have good meat but less of it. St. Louis ribs have much more meat and great flavor.

MAKES ABOUT 9 SERVINGS

3 racks St. Louis cut spare ribs

½ cup (60 ml) prepared mustard

1½ cups (344 g) cold unsalted butter, sliced

½ cup (60 ml) honey

1 cup (100 g) Memphis dry rub

¾ cup (180 ml) apple cider

MEMPHIS DRY RUB

¼ cup (48 g) turbinado sugar

2 tbsp (20 g) paprika

1 tbsp (6 g) chili powder

1 tbsp (7 g) freshly ground black pepper

1 tbsp (18 g) kosher salt

2 tsp (4 g) ground cumin

2 tsp (1 g) dried oregano

1 tsp garlic powder

½ tsp cayenne pepper

Remove the outer membranes on the bone side of the ribs. There will be two membranes. The one attached closest to the bone and meat stays. The outer, thicker membrane is removed by grasping it with a paper towel and peeling it from the bone tips down to where the flap was. The membrane removal works best if the ribs are very cold. Sometimes during the butchering process, the membrane has already been removed, so don't stress out trying to remove something that isn't there. (I speak from experience!) On the meat side of the ribs, remove any thick fat pieces that you may find between the bones. Also remove the layer of fat and sinew on the short bone end of the rack, exposing the rib meat. Trim any meat hanging from the end of the cut bones to give a very even appearance. Once trimmed, rub the racks with yellow mustard and then rub with pork rub on both sides. These can be wrapped and placed in the refrigerator for a few hours until ready to cook.

Set the Egg for 250°F (120°C) indirect with a drip pan. The fire box should be almost full with charcoal. With the top and bottom vents wide open, light the fire and close the Egg. When the Egg gets up to about 250°F (121°C) dome, about 10 minutes, close the bottom screen. When the Egg approaches 250°F (120°C) dome, slide the top of the daisy wheel closed, leaving the petals halfway open. Once the fire is lit, add two chunks of maple and one chunk of fruitwood, apple, cherry or peach. Once the smoke has settled down to a bluish-gray color, add the ribs either bone-side down on the grate side by side, or on their sides in a vertical rib rack. Use an extended grate for 2 layers if the racks don't fit flat on the grate. Cook for 3 hours, turning and rotating every 45 minutes. (Do not flip the slabs if they are lying flat on the grate, just

(continued)

rotate them). If using a rib rack, rotate the ribs and flip them in the rack every hour. After 3 hours, place the racks on a double layer of aluminum foil, meat-side down. The foil should have a layer of butter, drizzled honey and sprinkles of rub. Wrap each rack tightly in the foil and add ¼ cup (60 ml) of apple juice prior to wrapping completely. Place foiled ribs back on the 250° (121°C) Egg, meat-side down and stacked, if necessary, for another hour. Rotate and change the stacking order a couple of times. After an hour, the wrapped ribs should be very limber when held by the ends. Remove from the foil and place on the grate, meat-side down, and add a thin layer of rub. Flip when rubbed and rub the meat side. Leave on the Egg for 15 or 20 minutes for the rub to melt and caramelize.

Once finished, let the cooked ribs rest, tented in foil on a drying rack for about 10 minutes. To cut, place them meat-side down on a cutting board and slice between the bones. Slicing them bone-side up allows you to see the bones better, as they will change direction farther down the slab. Serve meat-side up.

I prefer to eat pork ribs "dry," with no sauce in the cooking process, as opposed to "wet," in which the ribs are basted in sauce. You will taste more pork flavor dry. Sauce can always be served on the side. Most of the KCBS judges say they like dry ribs better, but the one time we turned them in dry, they didn't do well. For KCBS, most teams turn in sauced ribs.

Removing the membrane.

Applying mustard before the rub.

Sprinkling the rub.

CAJUN PORK STEAKS

I've said it before: I think that pork butts are the best and most versatile part of the pig, even better than bacon. Pork steaks are sliced, bone-in pork butts. They are like giant pork chops, but juicier and more tender. Ask your butcher to slice a whole pork butt for you. They are the tastiest and cheapest part of the pig...a twofer!

MAKES ABOUT 4 SERVINGS

CAJUN RUB

2 tbsp (20 g) paprika

1 tbsp (12 g) dark brown sugar

1 tbsp (18 g) kosher salt

2 tsp (4.5 g) freshly ground black pepper

2 tsp (4 g) ground white pepper

2 tsp (4 g) cayenne pepper

2 tsp (4 g) garlic powder

2 tsp (4 g) onion powder

2 tsp (1 g) dried oregano

1 tsp thyme

1 tsp dry mustard

4 pork steaks, cut from the butt, ½-inch (1.3-cm) thick, about 2–3 lb (900 g–1.3 kg)

2 tbsp (30 ml) prepared yellow mustard

1 cup (237 ml) apple cider or apple juice

Set the Egg for 250°F (120°C) indirect with a drip pan. With the top and bottom vents wide open, light the fire and close the Egg. When the Egg gets up to about 250°F (121°C) dome, about 10 minutes, close the bottom screen and slide the top of the daisy wheel closed, with the petals half open. In a small bowl, mix all of the Cajun rub spices together. Wipe any bone sawdust off the steaks and pat dry. Slather them with mustard and then add the Cajun rub to each steak. When the Egg is up to temperature, place the steaks on the grate and cook until they reach an internal temperature of 200°F (93°C), about 1 hour. Turn and flip the steaks every half hour, and spray them with apple cider to keep them moist. When the steaks are done, remove them from the Egg and let them rest for 10 minutes, tented under aluminum foil. Serve!

CHAR SIU BARBECUED PORK TENDERLOIN

Char Siu (Cha Shao) is a Cantonese barbecued pork that is popular all over Asia.
The pork is sweet, sticky, savory and a little spicy. As an alternative, you can use 1-inch (2.5-cm)
wide slices of pork butt or pork belly. Now I'm hungry!

MAKES ABOUT 6 SERVINGS

MARINADE

½ cup (120 ml) soy sauce

5 tbsp (75 ml) rice wine vinegar

2 tbsp (30 ml) vegetable oil

1 tbsp (12 g) dark brown sugar

¼ tsp five spice powder

1 tsp freshly ground black pepper

1 tbsp (10 g) fresh garlic, minced

1 tbsp (10 g) fresh ginger, minced

2 pork tenderloins

2 tbsp (30 ml) olive oil

½ tsp ground black pepper

1 tsp kosher salt

In a large bowl, mix all of the marinade ingredients together. Remove any visible fat or silver skin from the tenderloins. Place the whole tenderloins in a 1-gallon (3.8-L) resealable plastic bag and pour in the marinade. Refrigerate for 2 to 6 hours, massaging occasionally.

Set the Egg for high heat, 500°F (260°C), direct. With the top and bottom vents wide open, light the fire and close the Egg. When the Egg gets up to about 250°F (121°C) dome, about 10 minutes, close the bottom screen. When the Egg approaches 500°F (260°C) dome, about 10 to 15 minutes, slide the top of the daisy wheel partially closed, leaving it halfway open. Remove the tenderloins from the marinade and allow them to come up to room temperature, about 20 minutes. Rub them with olive oil and sprinkle them with salt and pepper. When the Egg is up to temperature, sear the tenderloins for one or two minutes per side on all four sides. Remove the tenderloins and reduce the temperature of the Egg to 350°F to 375°F (180°C to 190°C) by closing the daisy wheel top to a quarter of the way open for about 10 to 15 minutes. Return the meat to the Egg and continue cooking, turning a few times, until the internal temperature reaches 135°F (57°C), about 15 minutes. Do not overcook. Remove from the Egg, cover with foil and let rest for 10 minutes. The internal temperature should rise to 145°F (63°C). Cut into ½-inch (1.5-cm) slices and serve hot or cold.

MOLASSES AND BROWN SUGAR FLAVORED BRINED PORK CHOPS

Most everyone I know grew up eating pork chops. They were usually pan fried, crisp on the outside and a little dry on the inside. For the past couple of decades, pork has become leaner and leaner. Chops now have very little fat, making them dry when cooked. By using brine, the moisture is retained in the chop, making them more tender and juicy. Do not leave them in the brine too long, or they will end up tough and salty. Along with the salt in the brine, you can also infuse other flavors into the chop at the same time. Consider adding other spices to give different flavors.

MAKES ABOUT 4 SERVINGS

3 cups (720 ml) cold water

¼ cup (72 g) kosher salt

½ cup (100 g) dark brown sugar

½ tsp vanilla extract

2 tbsp (30 ml) dark molasses

½ tsp cayenne pepper

1 cup (240 ml) ice cubes

4 bone-in loin rib chops, 1½-inch (4-cm) thick, about 3 lb (1.4 kg)

2 tbsp (30 ml) olive oil

¼ cup (50 g) pork rub

Make the brine by boiling 1 cup (240 ml) water, then adding the salt, sugar, vanilla extract, molasses and cayenne pepper, stirring to dissolve. Add the remaining water and the ice cubes. Refrigerate the brine for at least 1 hour, until it is about 42° F (5.5° C). Rinse the chops and pat them dry, removing any bone saw dust. Three to 4 hours before cook time, place the chops and the cold brine in a resealable 2-gallon (7.8-L) freezer bag. Refrigerate for 3 to 4 hours, turning every half hour. You can remove the chops from the brine and store them wrapped in plastic wrap for up to a day in the refrigerator before cooking.

Set the Egg for 450°F (230°C) direct. With the top and bottom vents wide open, light the fire and close the Egg. When the Egg gets up to about 250° F (121° C) dome, about 10 minutes, close the bottom screen. When the Egg approaches 450°F (230° C) dome, about 10 to 15 minutes, slide the top of the daisy wheel partially closed, leaving it halfway open. After 3 to 4 hours in the brine, remove the chops and rinse, then pat them dry. Coat with olive oil, then rub with pork rub. When the Egg is up to temperature, sear the chops for 3 minutes per side until caramelized. Remove the chops and set up the Egg for 350°F (180°C) indirect with a drip pan. When the Egg is back down to 350°F (180°C), place the chops back on and grill for 6 minutes, flipping once until the internal temperature reaches 135°F (57°C). Remove from the Egg and tent in aluminum foil on a rack to rest for 10 minutes. The rested internal temperature should read between 145°F and 150°F (63°C and 66°C).

JERK PORK BUTT

Jerk seasoning is well rooted in Jamaica and is both spicy and aromatic. It is most commonly used for chicken and pork. This recipe uses a "flattened" boneless pork butt. It is marinated in the jerk paste before being cooked. Scotch bonnet and habanero peppers can be hot. If it is too spicy, next time you can cut back on the peppers or use a milder jalapeño or serrano pepper with the seeds and ribs removed.

MAKES ABOUT 6 TO 8 SERVINGS

1 or 2 scotch bonnet or habanero peppers, seeded and chopped

1 cup (151 g) onion, chopped

½ cup (20 g) green onion, chopped

1 tsp dried thyme

½ tbsp (9 g) kosher salt

1 tbsp (6 g) ground allspice

½ tsp ground nutmeg

1 tsp ground cinnamon

2 tsp (4.5 g) freshly ground black pepper

2 tsp (19 g) garlic, minced

2 tbsp (30 ml) vegetable oil

5 to 6 lb (2.2 to 2.7 kg) fresh boneless pork butt

In a food processor, mix all of the ingredients except the pork into a paste. Lay the pork butt fat-side down and remove any visible sinew or large pieces of fat. Spread three-quarters of the jerk paste into the butt. Place the butt, meat-side down, in a glass casserole dish and rub the remaining jerk paste into the fat side. Cover with plastic wrap and marinate in the refrigerator for 2 to 8 hours.

Set the Egg for 350°F (180°C) indirect with a drip pan. With the top and bottom vents wide open, light the fire and close the Egg. When the Egg gets up to about 250°F (121°C) dome, about 10 minutes, close the bottom screen. When the Egg approaches 350°F (180°C) dome, about 10 minutes, slide the top of the daisy wheel partially closed, leaving it a quarter of the way open. Remove the pork from the dish and wipe off most of the marinade. Bring the pork up to room temperature for about 20 minutes. Prior to adding the meat, put in three chunks of apple or cherry wood. Initially, there will be very white, billowy smoke. This is bad, bitter smoke! Wait until the smoke has settled down to a bluish-gray color and add the butt to the grate, fat side up. Cook at 350°F (180°C) until the internal temperature reaches 190°F to 195°F (88°C to 91°C), about 1 hour.

Remove the pork from the Egg and let rest under a foil tent for about 10 minutes. When rested, cut into 1-inch (2.5-cm) chunks and serve.

CANDIED PORK BELLY

Fresh pork belly can be cooked for the best combination of mildly spicy pork flavor with a very soft, creamy texture. We made this recipe for NewEGGland Fest this past summer and it was a huge hit. Fresh pork belly can be found at Asian markets, or your supermarket's meat manager may be able to order it for you. If you can only find skin on pork belly, remove the skin, salt and grill for cracklins. I'll make a bet that no one can eat these bites and not smile by the time the toothpick is cleaned off!

MAKES ABOUT 10 SERVINGS

---

3 lb (1.4 kg) fresh skinless, boneless pork belly

48 wooden toothpicks

MARINADE

1 cup (240 ml) orange juice

1 cup (240 ml) pineapple juice

½ cup (120 ml) lime juice

¼ cup (60 ml) olive oil

¼ cup (60 ml) pure maple syrup

2 tsp (6 g) minced garlic

½ tsp salt

½ tsp freshly ground black pepper

RUB

2 tbsp (23 g) brown sugar

1 tsp ground cinnamon

1 tsp ground nutmeg

Pinch cayenne pepper

Rinse the pork belly in cold water and pat dry. In a large bowl, mix the marinade ingredients. Place the belly and the marinade in a resealable plastic bag. Refrigerate for 12 to 24 hours, flipping and massaging all the sides occasionally. Once marinated, remove from the bag, pat dry and let the belly come up to room temperature, about 30 minutes.

Set up the Egg for 300°F (150°C) indirect with a drip pan. With the top and bottom vents wide open, light the fire and close the Egg. When the Egg gets up to about 250°F (121°C) dome, about 10 minutes, close the bottom screen. When the Egg approaches 300°F (150°C) dome, about 5 minutes, slide the top of the daisy wheel closed, leaving the petals all of the way open. When the Egg is up to temperature, place the belly in a roasting pan, or a disposable aluminum half pan and place on the Egg, cover and roast until the internal temperature of the belly reaches 200°F (93°C), about 2 hours. When the pork belly is cooked, let it rest for about half an hour.

While the belly is resting, mix the rub ingredients together in a small bowl. Increase the temperature of the Egg to 375°F (190°C). Once the belly has rested, cut it into 1-inch (2.5-cm) thick slices, and then cut each of the slices into 1-inch (2.5-cm) pieces. Sprinkle each piece with the rub and place a toothpick through the top of each. Place the pork pieces on the grate, on their sides, and rotate every 30 seconds until the brown sugar has caramelized on each side, but not burned. Remove from the Egg and serve.

FIVE SPICE BABY BACK RIBS

When I go out to eat, I prefer to eat Chinese food. I usually get the boneless spare ribs because I like the flavor. I know that they are not really ribs, but I like the marinade flavors. This recipe produces both the pork flavor of the baby backs and the marinade flavors I enjoy. These aren't "barbecued," but they are great for a change of pace.

MAKES ABOUT 4 SERVINGS

MARINADE

½ cup (120 ml) dark soy sauce

½ cup (120 ml) dry sherry

2 tbsp (23 g) dark brown sugar

2 tbsp (29 g) fresh ginger, minced

1 tbsp (15 ml) sesame oil

2 tsp (6 g) fresh garlic, minced

1 tsp five spice powder

½ tsp freshly ground black pepper

¼ tsp ground white pepper

2 racks of baby back ribs, each cut into two rib sections

In a small bowl, mix all of the marinade ingredients together. Place the marinade in a re-sealable plastic bag and add the cut up baby backs. Mix the ribs with the marinade and lay the bag in a casserole dish, refrigerating for 8 to 10 hours, turning often.

Set the Egg for 350°F (180°C) indirect with a drip pan. With the top and bottom vents wide open, light the fire and close the Egg. When the Egg gets up to about 250°F (121°C) dome, about 10 minutes, close the bottom screen. When the Egg approaches 350°F (180°C) dome, about 10 minutes, slide the top of the daisy wheel partially closed, leaving it a quarter of the way open. Remove the ribs from the marinade and allow them to come up to room temperature, about 15 minutes. Place the used marinade in a saucepan and simmer for about 10 minutes.

When the Egg is up to temperature, place the ribs on the grate and cook until they reach an internal temperature of 160°F (71°C), about 30 to 40 minutes. Turn and flip the ribs every 10 minutes and brush them with the simmered marinade. When the ribs are up to about 160°F (71°C) internal, remove the drip pan and plate setter for a direct setup. Grill the ribs 3 to 4 minutes per side to get a little char color and flavor, then remove them from the Egg and let them rest for 10 minutes, tented under aluminum foil. Serve!

MY FAVORITE BRATWURST FATTIE

My recipe uses the bratwurst flavorings in a fattie roll. I have also added sauerkraut
and beer to up the bratwurst flavor. Slice and serve the bratwurst in a hamburger bun,
topped with mustard and grilled onion slices.

EACH 1 POUND (448 G) FATTIE MAKES ABOUT 8 TO 10 SERVINGS

---

2 lb (900 g) pork shoulder, bone removed, 80/20 mix meat to fat

1 lb (448 g) veal

½ cup (120 ml) whole milk

2 eggs, beaten

¼ cup (60 ml) dark beer

1 tbsp (18 g) kosher salt

2 tsp (2 g) finely ground white pepper

1 tsp nutmeg

1 tsp mace

½ tsp ground ginger

GRILLED ONIONS

2 large onions

2 tbsp (30 ml) olive oil

2 tsp (12 g) kosher salt

1 tsp freshly ground black pepper

Cut the pork shoulder and the veal into 1-inch (2.5-cm) strips, removing only silver skin and cartilage. Using a coarse grind plate, grind the pork and the veal, a few pieces at a time. Alternate grinding several pieces of pork with a few pieces of the veal to get a good mix.

In a large bowl, add the remainder of the ingredients and whisk them together, then mix them gently by hand with half of the ground meat. You can tell that the spices are mixed in well by a uniform pattern in the bowl. Don't oversqueeze the meat, as it will make the sausage more dry. Add the remainder of the ground meat to the bowl and mix gently.

Form the finished sausage into three 1-pound (450-g) logs, about 2 inches (5 cm) in diameter. Place one log at the end of long piece of plastic wrap and begin to roll the log, keeping it tight as you roll. When complete, there should be no air pockets and the roll should be firm to the touch. Roll the remaining 2 logs. Refrigerate the meat for half an hour. If you're not using all of the meat for this cook, it can be placed in a resealable plastic freezer bag and frozen for later use.

Set the Egg for 350°F (180°C), indirect with a drip pan. With the top and bottom vents wide open, light the fire and close the Egg. When the Egg gets up to about 250°F (121°C) dome, about 10 minutes, close the bottom screen. When the Egg approaches 350°F (180°C) dome, about 10 minutes, slide the top of the daisy wheel partially closed, leaving it a quarter of the way open. Remove the log, now a fattie, from the plastic wrap and coat with salt and pepper. Place the fattie on the Egg, close the dome and cook for 30 minutes until the internal temperature reaches 160°F (71°C). Remove from the heat, tent with foil and let rest for 10 minutes before slicing into ½-inch (1.3-cm) slices.

Slice the onion into ½-inch (1.3-cm) slices. Rub the slices with olive oil and sprinkle them with salt and pepper. While the fatties are cooking, place the onions on the same oiled grate and cook for about 5 minutes per side, turning once. As an alternative, use mustard instead of olive oil, salt and pepper. They may not char, but they will be good! Let them cook longer if you like a darker onion.

NORTH CAROLINA PORK BUTT WITH EASTERN VINEGAR PEPPER SAUCE

North Carolina is well known for its pulled pork. The debate is whether the sauce is better in the eastern or western part of the state. This eastern sauce is a simple vinegar and crushed red pepper combination. It is not very sweet and it does not have any tomato in it. Though called a sauce, it is more liquid than a paste, and is used for mopping, dressing the pulled or chopped pork or as a dipping sauce. This sauce is simple, as is the rub for the butt—just oil, salt and pepper. The cooking time is long, but the smells are intoxicating.

MAKES ABOUT 15 SERVINGS

EASTERN VINEGAR PEPPER SAUCE

2 cups (480 ml) cider vinegar

1 cup (240 ml) white vinegar

2 tbsp (23 g) light brown sugar

1 tbsp (5 g) crushed red pepper flakes

1 tsp freshly ground black pepper

1 tsp kosher salt

1 (7 to 8 lb [3.2 to 3.7 kg]) bone-in pork butt

¼ cup (60 ml) olive oil

2 tbsp (36 g) kosher salt

2 tbsp (14 g) freshly ground black pepper

Set the Egg for 300°F (150°C) indirect with a drip pan. With the top and bottom vents wide open, light the fire and close the Egg. When the Egg gets up to about 250°F (121°C) dome, about 10 minutes, close the bottom screen. When the Egg approaches 300°F (150°C) dome, about 5 minutes, slide the top of the daisy wheel closed, leaving the petals fully open. Prior to adding the meat, put in 3 chunks of maple, pecan or applewood. Initially, there will be very white, billowy smoke. This is bad, bitter smoke! Wait until the smoke has settled down to a bluish-gray color.

Mix all of the sauce ingredients together in a large bowl. Pat the butt dry and check the bottom for any shards of bone. Rub the butt with olive oil and sprinkle with salt and pepper. When the Egg is up to temperature, place the butt on the grate, fat-side up, and cook to an internal temperature of 190°F (88°C), about 6 to 8 hours. Rotate the butt every hour and mop with sauce. When the butt is done, remove it from the Egg and wrap it in aluminum foil. Put the butt in a warm place to rest for at least an hour. When ready to serve, pull the cooked pork apart, discarding any sinew or cartilage. Pull it into small pieces or chop it. Add the sauce and mix thoroughly. Serve on a plate or in a bun with slaw.

ADOBO RIBS WITH RUM GLAZE

I like barbecued pork ribs most any way I have them. This adobo recipe marinates the slabs in a garlic-and-citrus spice mixture, adding additional flavors to the pork. Adobo marinades can differ slightly by region, using vinegar, chili peppers and bitter oranges. You can experiment as you choose. The rum glaze used to finish the ribs is sticky, sweet and a little spicy.

MAKES ABOUT 6 SERVINGS

MARINADE

¾ cup (180 ml) lime juice

¾ cup (180 ml) orange juice

2 tbsp (30 ml) extra-virgin olive oil

2 tbsp (20 g) garlic, chopped

1 tbsp (2.5 g) fresh cilantro, chopped

1 tsp ground cumin

½ tsp kosher salt

½ tsp black pepper

½ tsp dried oregano

2 racks St. Louis cut spare ribs

2 tbsp (30 ml) olive oil

2 tsp (12 g) kosher salt

2 tsp (5 g) freshly ground black pepper

2 (½ cup [120 ml]) sticks unsalted butter, sliced

½ cup (50 g) honey

¾ cup (180 ml) apple cider

GLAZE

1 cup (240 ml) marinade, reserved after ribs have marinated

¼ cup (60 ml) dark rum

¼ cup (60 g) turbinado sugar

In a large bowl, whisk the liquid marinade ingredients together, then mix in the other ingredients until well blended. Refrigerate until ready to use. Remove the outer membranes on the bone side of the ribs. There will be 2 membranes. The one attached closest to the bone and meat stays. The outer, thicker membrane is removed by grasping it with a paper towel and peeling it from the bone tips down to where the flap was. The membrane removal works best if the ribs are very cold. Sometimes during the butchering process, the membrane has already been removed, so don't stress out trying to remove something that isn't there. (I speak from experience!) On the meat side of the ribs, remove any thick fat pieces that you may find between the bones. Also remove the layer of fat and sinew on the short bone end of the rack, exposing the rib meat. Trim any meat hanging from the end of the cut bones to give an even appearance. Once trimmed, place the ribs meat-side down in a large ceramic baking dish or a large resealable plastic bag and add the marinade. You may need to cut the racks in half to fit. Place in the refrigerator for 2 to 4 hours, until ready to cook.

Set the Egg for 250°F (121°C) indirect with a drip pan. The fire box should be almost full of charcoal. With the top and bottom vents wide open, light the fire and close the Egg. When the Egg gets up to about 250°F (121°C) dome, about 10 minutes, close the bottom screen and slide the top of the daisy wheel closed, leaving the petals halfway open. Once the fire is lit, add 2 chunks of maple and 1 chunk of fruitwood, apple, cherry or peach. Remove the ribs from the marinade and reserve 1 cup (240 ml) of the marinade. Coat the ribs with olive oil, salt and pepper and let them come up to room temperature. Once the smoke has settled down to a bluish-gray color, add the ribs either bone-side down on the grate side by side, or on their thin side in a vertical rib rack. Cook for 3 hours, turning and rotating every 45 minutes. (Do not flip the slabs if they are lying flat on the grate, just rotate them.)

Prepare the glaze by combining all of the ingredients in a saucepan and simmering until reduced by half.

After 3 hours, place the racks on a double layer of aluminum foil, meat-side down. Butter the foil and drizzle it with honey. Wrap each rack in the foil and add ¼ cup (60 ml) of apple juice prior to sealing. Place foiled ribs back on the 250°F (120°C) Egg, meat-side down and stacked, if necessary, for another hour. Rotate and change the stacking order a couple of times. After an hour, the wrapped ribs should be very limber when held by the ends. Remove from the foil and place on the grate, meat-side down, and glaze the bottom. Flip when glazed and glaze the meat side. Leave on the Egg for 15 or 20 minutes for the sauce to set. If you don't have grid space for all of the racks, remove them in pairs from the foil and sauce them two at a time until they are all glazed. Using an extended rack will allow you to glaze 4 racks at a time in a large Big Green Egg.

Once glazed, let the cooked ribs rest, tented in foil, on a drying rack for about 10 minutes. To cut, place them meat-side down on a cutting board and slice between the bones. Slicing them bone-side up allows you to see the bones better, as they will change direction farther down the slab. Serve meat-side up.

SHORT RIBS, PIG STYLE

This recipe takes St. Louis style pork ribs and cuts the slabs lengthwise to make "short ribs." They cook a little faster than full slabs and are great for appetizers. This recipe calls for turbinado sugar sprinkled and served dry, i.e., no barbecue sauce. Sauce is good, but I hope these ribs will bring you over to the dry side!

MAKES ABOUT 12 SERVINGS

2 racks St. Louis style ribs, sliced lengthwise into 1½-inch to 2½-inch (3.8- to 6.4-cm) strips. This will create 4 long racks of ribs, each 1½-inch to 2½-inch (3.8- to 6.4-cm) wide

¼ cup (60 ml) prepared yellow mustard

1 cup (100 g) pork rub

Butter, honey and additional rub for the foil

¼ cup (60 ml) apple juice

½ cup (125 g) turbinado sugar

To prepare, remove the membrane from the bone side of the rack. You can cut the racks yourself or ask your butcher to cut them for you before purchase. Remove any bone dust. Trim any meat hanging from the end of the cut bones to give an even appearance. Once trimmed, rub the racks with yellow mustard, then rub with pork rub on both sides. These can be wrapped and placed in the refrigerator for a few hours until ready to cook.

Set the Egg for 250°F (121°C) indirect with a drip pan. The fire box should be almost full of charcoal. With the top and bottom vents wide open, light the fire and close the Egg. When the Egg gets up to about 250°F (121°C) dome, about 10 minutes, close the bottom screen and slide the top of the daisy wheel closed, leaving the petals halfway open. Once the fire is lit, add 2 chunks of maple and 1 chunk of fruitwood, apple, cherry or peach. Once the smoke has settled down to a bluish-gray color, add the ribs either bone-side down on the grate side by side, or on thin side in a vertical rib rack.

(continued)

SHORT RIBS, PIG STYLE (CONT.)

Cook for 2 hours, turning and rotating every 30 minutes. (Do not flip the slabs if they are lying flat on the grate, just rotate them.) After 2 hours, place the racks on a double layer of aluminum foil, meat-side down. The foil should be buttered, drizzled with honey and sprinkled with rub. Wrap each rack in the foil and add ¼ cup (60 ml) of apple juice prior to sealing. Place foiled ribs back on the 250°F (121°C) Egg, meat-side down and stacked, if necessary, for another hour. Rotate and change the stacking order a couple of times. After an hour, the wrapped ribs should be very limber when held by the ends. Remove from the foil and place on the grate, meat-side up, and sprinkle with turbinado sugar. Leave on the Egg for 15 or 20 minutes for the rub to set. If you don't have grid space for all the racks, remove them in pairs from the foil and rub them two at a time until they are all covered. Using an extended rack will allow you to rub 4 racks at a time in a large Big Green Egg.

Once covered, let the cooked ribs rest, tented in foil on a drying rack for about 10 minutes. To cut, place them meat-side down on a cutting board and slice between the bones. Slicing them bone-side up allows you to see the bones better, as they will change direction farther down the slab. Serve meat-side up.

Removing the membrane.

Sprinkling on the rub.

Slicing the cooked ribs.

ASIAN BACON

Making your own pork belly bacon is easy to do and you have control of the flavors you add to it. This recipe is for Asian bacon. You can add spices to your dry cure to make it spicier or more savory. Try making a brown sugar–or pepper-flavored cure. Fresh pork belly can be found at Asian markets, or your supermarket's meat manager may be able to order it for you. Making your own cured, smoked bacon will elevate your neighborhood culinary stature, with minimal effort! You get to choose the flavors, the amount of smoke and how thick or thin to slice it. You will be a bacon bigwig in no time!

MAKES ABOUT 9 SERVINGS

3 lb (1.4 kg) fresh skinless, boneless pork belly

3 tbsp (45 g) Morton's Tenderquick® (curing agent)

1 tbsp (15 ml) fish sauce

1 tbsp (15 ml) soy sauce

1 tbsp (12 g) brown sugar

2 tsp (4 g) five spice powder

2 tsp (4 g) ginger powder

2 tsp (4 g) garlic powder

½ tbsp (3 g) freshly ground black pepper

¼ tsp crushed red pepper flakes

Rinse the pork belly in cold water and pat dry. Fill the fire box about one-third full. In a small bowl, mix the remaining ingredients together to form a well-mixed paste. Rub the paste in and on all sides of the pork belly. Place in a resealable plastic bag or in a vacuum-sealed bag. Refrigerate between 36°F and 40°F (2.2°C and 4.4°C) for 6 days, flipping and massaging all the sides once a day. Once cured, remove from the bag and rinse off thoroughly, rubbing the water into the belly.

Set up the Egg for 200°F (93°C) indirect with a drip pan. With the top and bottom vents wide open, light the fire and close the Egg. When the Egg gets up to about 200°F (93°C) dome, about 10 minutes, close the bottom screen and slide the top of the daisy wheel closed, leaving the petals a little less than a quarter open. Add 3 fruit wood chunks and place the pork belly on a raised grid, up in the dome. Smoke until the internal temperature of the pork reaches 160°F (71°C), about 2 hours. When the pork belly is cooked, let it rest for about half an hour before refrigerating or freezing.

Your homemade bacon is easier to slice after it is refrigerated. You can also slice it before freezing it in 1 pound (450 g) bags.

SOUTHWESTERN CHORIZO PATTIES

Chorizo is a sausage with both Spanish and Mexican variations. It's spicy and is great when freshly made into patties. I have had store-bought chorizo in casings, which was more chopped and much drier. I like the patties because of their flavor and juiciness. As an alternative, you can replace one half of the pork with ground beef chuck, but try to keep an 80% to 20% meat-to-fat ratio.

MAKES ABOUT 12 SERVINGS

3 lb (1.4 kg) pork shoulder, bone removed. If you don't have a grinder, ask your butcher to grind it for you

½ cup (100 g) minced onion

⅓ cup (78 ml) vinegar

1 cup (200 g) chopped jalapeños, seeds and ribs removed

2 tsp (4 g) ground cumin

1 tsp dried oregano

2 tbsp (12 g) chili powder

1 tbsp (18 g) kosher salt

1 tsp freshly ground black pepper

½ tsp cinnamon

1 tsp cayenne pepper

½ tsp ground coriander

Cut the pork shoulder into 1- by 1-inch (2.5- by 2.5-cm) strips, removing silver skin and cartilage. Using a coarse grind plate, grind the pork a few pieces at a time. If you don't have access to a grinder, ask your butcher to grind it for you. In a separate bowl, mix all the remaining ingredients together, then mix half of the ground meat into the bowl by hand. Don't oversqueeze the meat. Add the remainder of the meat to the bowl and gently mix.

For best results, refrigerate the mix for 12 hours or overnight to let the flavors meld. Remove from the refrigerator and form patties.

Set the Egg for 350°F (180°C) indirect with a drip pan. With the top and bottom vents wide open, light the fire and close the Egg. When the Egg gets up to about 250°F (121°C) dome, about 10 minutes, close the bottom screen. When the Egg approaches 350°F (180°C) dome, about 10 minutes, slide the top of the daisy wheel partially closed, leaving it a quarter of the way open. Place the patties on the Egg and cook for 20 minutes, until the internal temperature reaches 165°F (74°). Remove from heat, tent with foil and let rest for 5 minutes before serving.

As an alternative, the chorizo mix can be crumbled into an oiled grill pan and browned to be used in omelets, salads and tacos.

FRUITY PORK LOIN

Pork loin is basically a huge, boneless pork chop. The white meat is very lean and doesn't have a great deal of flavor. By utilizing flavorful brine, moisture and flavors are retained in the roast. Adding a fruit glaze near the end of the cook pairs very well with the pork.

MAKES 6 TO 8 SERVINGS

BRINE

2 cups (480 ml) cold water

2 tbsp (36 g) kosher salt

½ cup (100 g) granulated sugar

¼ cup (60 ml) orange juice

2 tbsp (20 g) crushed garlic

1 tbsp (7 g) black peppercorns

1 (4 lb [1.8 kg]) boneless pork loin, from blade end if possible

2 tbsp (30 ml) olive oil

¼ cup (30 g) pork rub

GLAZE

1 cup (240 ml) apricot or peach jelly

¼ cup (60 ml) soy sauce

2 tsp (10 ml) olive oil

Place ½ cup (120 ml) of the water in a microwave-safe bowl and add the salt and sugar. Heat it in the microwave until dissolved, about 5 minutes. Once dissolved, add the remaining water, orange juice, garlic and peppercorns and stir to combine.

Remove any visible sinew or silver skin from the pork, and then place it in a resealable plastic bag with the brine. Refrigerate in the brine for 4 to 6 hours.

To prepare the glaze, add all of the ingredients to a small saucepan and simmer until blended.

Set up the Egg for 350°F (180°C) indirect with a drip pan. With the top and bottom vents wide open, light the fire and close the Egg. When the Egg gets up to about 250°F (121°C) dome, about 10 minutes, close the bottom screen. When the Egg approaches 350°F (180°C) dome, about 10 minutes, slide the top of the daisy wheel partially closed, leaving it a quarter of the way open. Remove the loin from the brine, rinse and pat it dry. Coat with olive oil, then rub with pork rub. Let the loin come up to room temperature, about 15 minutes.

When the Egg is up to temperature, place the loin on the grate and cook until the internal temperature reaches 140°F (60°C), about 60 minutes. During the last 15 minutes of the cook, brush the loin on all sides with the glaze. When cooked, remove from the Egg and tent in aluminum foil on a rack to rest for 10 minutes. The rested internal temperature should read between 145°F and 150°F (63°C and 66°C). Slice into 1-inch (2.5-cm) slices and serve.

BOURBON COUNTRY STYLE PORK RIBS

Around here, "country style" pork ribs are not ribs at all. They are either cut from the loin area (less red, more pink and white) or from the shoulder area (more red, less pink, more fat). I greatly prefer the "ribs" cut from the shoulder than the loin. They are more flavorful and less dry. If you don't see them in the meat case, ask your meat man to slice a pork butt into 1- to 1½-inch (2.5- to 4-cm) thick "ribs." The marinade will flavor the pork with the sweetness of the bourbon, cola and sugar; the simple salt and pepper; and the added background flavors of the bourbon and cola. When grilled, the bark on the outside will add an additional spicy flavor and texture.

MAKES ABOUT 8 SERVINGS

MARINADE

½ cup (120 ml) bourbon

¼ cup (60 ml) cola

¼ cup (60 ml) dark soy sauce

¼ cup (45 g) dark brown sugar

¼ tsp kosher salt

½ tsp freshly ground black pepper

8 "country style" pork ribs

2 tbsp (30 ml) yellow mustard or vegetable oil

½ cup (60 g) pork rub

Mix all of the marinade ingredients together and refrigerate. Trim fat from the meat, leaving no more than ¼ inch (6 mm). Cut off any sinew or cartilage and check for bone chips. Place the pork in a resealable plastic freezer bag and add the marinade. Lay the bag flat in a casserole dish and refrigerate for 4 to 6 hours, flipping occasionally.

Remove the pork from the marinade, pat dry and coat with mustard or oil. Coat all sides of the meat with pork rub.

Set the Egg for 300°F (150°C), indirect with a drip pan. With the top and bottom vents wide open, light the fire and close the Egg. When the Egg gets up to about 250°F (121°C) dome, about 10 minutes, close the bottom screen. When the Egg approaches 300°F (150°C) dome, about 5 minutes, slide the top of the daisy wheel closed, leaving the petals open.

Cook ribs for about 1½ hours, turning occasionally. Internal temperature should be between 190°F and 200°F (88°C and 93°C). Remove from the Egg and tent under aluminum foil for 10 minutes before serving.

CROWN ROAST OF PORK

Crown roast is typically a holiday or large gathering endeavor. It takes a little time to prepare, but this brined recipe keeps the pork juicy. Although the presentation of a crown roast is usually the star here, it takes a backseat to flavor pork.

MAKES ABOUT 6 SERVINGS

STUFFING

½ lb (227 g) thick-sliced applewood smoked bacon, diced

1 medium onion, chopped

1 celery rib, diced

2 tsp (6 g) garlic, minced

Pinch freshly ground black pepper

1 cup (150 g) grated sweet potato

1 cup (150 g) bread crumbs

¼ cup (40 g) golden raisins or dried cranberries

1 (8 to 10 lb [3.6 to 4.5 kg]) bone-in loin rib roast, chine bone removed. Your butcher can cut the chine bone and bottom outside between every bone about a ½" (1.3 cm) for you before purchase so you can pull the roast into the crown shape

1 tbsp (15 ml) olive oil

½ cup (100 g) pork rub

Butcher twine

BRINE

4 cups (960 ml) cold water

½ cup (144 g) kosher salt

1 cup (200 g) brown sugar

2 cups (480 ml) cold apple cider or apple juice

In a saucepan using medium heat, cook the bacon until almost crisp, about 4 minutes, and remove it to paper towels to drain. Remove all but 2 tablespoons (30 ml) of the bacon fat from the skillet and sauté the onion, celery and garlic until translucent, about 4 minutes. Add the black pepper and the sweet potato and stir until the potato starts to soften, about 3 minutes. Pour the saucepan mixture into a large bowl, add the cool bacon, bread crumbs and raisins and mix until sticky. Add 2 tablespoons (30 ml) of the reserved bacon fat.

Slice the bottom outside of the roast between every other bone, about ½ inch (12 mm) deep. This will help when forming the crown before cooking. French the ends of the rib bones down about 2 inches (5 cm) by removing all of the meat and tissue between the bones.

At least 5 hours before cooking time, make the brine by boiling 1 cup (240 ml) water, then adding the salt and sugar, stirring to dissolve. Remove from the heat and let cool to room temperature. Add the remaining cold water and cold apple cider. Refrigerate the brine for at least one hour to bring the temperature safely down to 40°F (4°C). Rinse off the roast and pat dry, removing any silver skin from the bone side of the roast. Place the roast and the cold brine in a resealable 2-gallon (7.6-L) freezer bag. Refrigerate lying flat for 2 to 4 hours, turning every half hour.

Set up the Egg for 350°F (180°C) indirect with a drip pan. With the top and bottom vents wide open, light the fire and close the Egg. When the Egg gets up to about 250°F (121°C) dome, about 10 minutes, close the bottom screen. When the Egg approaches 350°F (180°C) dome, about 10 minutes, slide the top of the daisy wheel partially closed, leaving it a quarter of the way open.

Remove the roast from the brine, rinse, and then pat it dry. Form the crown by bending the 2 roast ends together, with the meat side facing out. Tie the crown with butcher twine in 2 circles to hold its shape. Rub the inside of the crown with olive oil and rub in the pork rub. Let the roast come up to room temperature, about 30 minutes from when it was removed from the marinade. When the Egg is up to temperature, place the crown on the grate and roast until the internal temperature reaches 140°F (60°C), about 2½ to 3 hours. About an hour before the roast is cooked, spoon the stuffing mixture into the center of the roast. Remove from the Egg and tent in aluminum foil on a rack to rest for 10 minutes. The rested internal temperature should read between 145°F and 150°F (63°C and 66°C).

PORCHETTA

Porchetta in its traditional form is a deboned, young pig filled with loin meat, garlic and herbs, tied and spit roasted. The cooked meat is very juicy and well flavored by the herbs. The crisp pig skin is chopped with the rest of the pig and served on its own or in sandwiches. There are many variations today, but all involve slow roasted pork stuffed with garlic and herbs.

The first time I had porchetta was at a BBQ contest in Harvard, Massachusetts. Jed LaBonte, the pitmaster of Uncle Jed's Barbecue Team, made it for his crew for an evening dinner. He used a butterflied pork shoulder. It was impressive! The variation I have uses a skin-on pork belly stuffed with a boneless pork loin. When it's finished, I serve it on ciabatta bread. It's juicy, herby and the textures go from soft to chewy to crunchy. It's great!

MAKES ABOUT 10 TO 12 SERVINGS

2 tbsp (18 g) garlic, minced

2 tbsp (5 g) fresh rosemary, chopped

2 tbsp (5 g) fresh sage leaves, chopped

2 tbsp (5 g) fresh thyme leaves, chopped

1 tbsp (18 g) kosher salt

2 tsp (5 g) freshly ground black pepper

2 tsp (1 g) red pepper flakes

4 tbsp (60 ml) olive oil

1 boneless, skin-on pork belly, 10-inch (25-cm) long, about 4 lb (1.8 kg)

1 (10-inch [25-cm]) piece of pork loin, about 3 lb (1.4 kg)

Butcher's twine

In a small bowl or food processor, mince the herbs and spices together, including 1 tablespoon (18 g) of the salt and 2 tablespoons (30 ml) of the olive oil. Lay the belly skin-side down and place the pork loin in the middle of it. To check for proper sizing, wrap the belly around the loin so that the two sides of the belly touch each other. If the belly is too long, trim it. If the loin is too big, trim it. When finished, lay out the belly skin-side down and score the meat in a diamond pattern, about ½ inch (12 mm)deep and 1 inch (2.5 cm) apart. Spread half of the herb mixture over the meat side of the belly, rubbing it into all the cuts. Butterfly the pork loin by cutting it almost all the way in half, leaving about ½ inch (12 mm) intact. Lay the loin open like a book. Rub the remaining half of the herb mixture on the inside of the loin. When finished, close the loin and place it in the middle of the meat side of the pork belly. Wrap the belly around the loin and tie it tightly with butcher twine every 1 inch (2.5 cm). Place the roll into the refrigerator for 24 hours, unwrapped, to let the meat marinate and the belly skin air-dry. About an hour before cooking time, remove the pork from the refrigerator and let it come up to room temperature.

Set the Egg for 350°F (180°C) indirect over a drip pan. With the top and bottom vents wide open, light the fire and close the Egg. When the Egg gets up to about 250°F (121°C) dome, about 10 minutes, close the bottom screen. When the Egg approaches 350°F (180°C) dome, about 10 minutes, slide the top of the daisy wheel partially closed, leaving it a quarter of the way open. Rub the belly skin with the remaining olive oil and salt. When the Egg is up to temperature, place the pork on the grate over the drip pan. Roast until the internal temperature is 140°F (60°C), about 1½ to 2 hours, rotating every 30 minutes. If the skin is not crisp, increase the temperature of the Egg to 500°F (260°C) by sliding the cover of the daisy wheel so it is half open, for about 10 minutes, until the skin is crispy.

Remove the pork, cover with foil and let rest for 15 to 20 minutes. The internal temperature should rise to 145°F (63°C). Cut into ½-inch (1.5-cm) slices and serve on a plate or on a ciabatta roll.

CHAPTER 3

GLAZED, GRILLED & ROASTED, TENDER & JUICY CHICKEN & TURKEY RECIPES FOR THE WHOLE FAMILY

Many people prefer to eat poultry over red meats. I prefer juicier dark meat over white meat, but white meat can be aided with brine and by making sure you don't overcook it. These recipes demonstrate how chicken and poultry can be grilled or smoked, and show off many different spices, glazes and marinades, explaining why poultry is so popular around the world. As with all foods cooked over charcoal, the hint of smoke adds the perfect flavor accent to chicken and turkey.

MARINATED MOJO SPATCHCOCK CHICKEN

A spatchcock chicken is a whole chicken with the backbone removed, so it lies flat when cooking and cooks more evenly. This recipe marinates the chicken in a Caribbean mojo marinade that is accented by citrus juice, cilantro, garlic and spices. The acidity in the juice will keep the chicken moist and tender, and the garlic will give a little pow! In short, it's got mojo!

MAKES ABOUT 4 SERVINGS

MARINADE

½ cup (60 ml) lime juice

½ cup (60 ml) orange juice

½ cup (20 g) cilantro, chopped

¼ cup (60 ml) olive oil

6 cloves garlic, minced

1 onion, chopped

½ cup (120 ml) dry sherry or white wine

1 tbsp (1.6 g) dried oregano

1 tsp cumin

1 tsp kosher salt

½ tsp black pepper

1 (4 to 5 lb [1.8 to 2.3 kg]) chicken, spatchcocked

In a medium bowl, mix all the marinade ingredients together. To spatchcock a whole chicken, wash it and pat it dry. Place the chicken breast-side down on a cutting board. Using a pair of kitchen or poultry shears, cut along one side of the backbone from the tail to the neck. Next, cut along the other side and remove the backbone. Press firmly down on both wing areas at the same time to break the breastbone. The chicken will now lie flat. Trim away any visible fat from the chicken. Place the spatchcocked chicken and the marinade in a resealable plastic freezer bag and lay the bag flat in a baking dish. If the chicken is too large to fit into a bag, marinate it in the baking dish with plastic wrap on top, and turn it often. Refrigerate the chicken and marinade for 4 to 6 hours.

Set the Egg for 375°F (190°C) indirect with a drip pan. With the top and bottom vents wide open, light the fire and close the Egg. When the Egg gets up to about 250°F (121°C) dome, about 10 minutes, close the bottom screen. When the Egg approaches 375°F (190°C) dome, about 10 minutes, slide the top of the daisy wheel partially closed, leaving it a quarter of the way open. Remove the chicken from the marinade and discard the marinade. Sprinkle the chicken with salt and pepper or your favorite chicken rub. When the Egg is up to temperature, place the chicken on the Egg and grill, turning it a few times, until the internal temperature reaches 165°F (74°C) in the thigh and breast, about 40 minutes. Let rest under tented aluminum foil on a rack for 5 minutes.

THAI CHICKEN THIGHS

These Thai chicken thighs will be sweet, sour and spicy all at the same time,
but no one element will overpower the others. Boneless thighs are good for this recipe
because they take the marinade well and will always be juicy and succulent.

MAKES ABOUT 6 SERVINGS

2 lb (900 g) boneless, skinless chicken thighs

¼ cup (10 g) freshly chopped cilantro

¼ cup (60 ml) honey

2 tsp (7 g) garlic, minced

1 tbsp (12 g) brown sugar

1 tbsp (15 g) ginger, grated

1 tbsp (15 ml) Asian fish sauce or soy sauce

1 tbsp (15 ml) vegetable oil

1 tsp Asian red chili paste

1 tsp freshly ground black pepper

1 tsp kosher salt

2 limes, cut into wedges

Check the thighs and remove any extra fat or pieces of gristle or bone. Combine all other ingredients, except the limes, in a large mixing bowl or food processor. Work the ingredients into a wet paste. Rub the paste all over the thighs and place them in a 1-gallon (3.8-L) resealable plastic bag. Let them marinate at least 4 hours or overnight, massaging the bag occasionally. Allow the thighs come to room temperature before grilling.

Set up the Egg for 325°F (160°C) indirect. With the top and bottom vents wide open, light the fire and close the Egg. When the Egg gets up to about 250°F (121°C) dome, about 10 minutes, close the bottom screen. When the Egg approaches 325°F (160°C) dome, about 10 minutes, slide the top of the daisy wheel partially closed, leaving it a quarter of the way open. Place the thighs on the grate, cut-side down, and grill until the internal temperature of all thighs reaches at least 165°F (74°C), about 20 to 30 minutes. When cooked, removed from the Egg and let rest, tented under foil, for about 5 minutes. Serve with lime wedges.

BROWN SUGAR GLAZED CHICKEN

Marinating the chicken helps retain moisture and adds flavor.
The chicken will be sweet, savory and a little spicy. A perfect balance of flavor.

MAKES ABOUT 4 SERVINGS

MARINADE

1¼ cups (251 g) brown sugar

1 tbsp (10 g) garlic, minced

3 tbsp (31 g) jalapeño pepper, diced

3 tbsp (45 ml) Worcestershire sauce

½ tsp salt

½ tsp black pepper

2 tsp (4.8 g) paprika

2 tbsp (30 ml) olive oil

½ tsp cayenne pepper

1 (3 to 4 lb [1.4 to 1.8 kg]) chicken, spatchcocked

Whisk all marinade ingredients together in a medium bowl. Place the marinade in a resealable plastic freezer bag and add the chicken. Massage the marinade around the chicken and lay the bag flat in a baking dish. If the chicken doesn't fit in the plastic bag, place it flat in a baking dish and cover it with plastic wrap. Refrigerate 4 hours, or overnight, turning 3 or 4 times.

Set the Egg for 375°F (190°C) indirect with a drip pan. With the top and bottom vents wide open, light the fire and close the Egg. When the Egg gets up to about 250°F (121°C) dome, about 10 minutes, close the bottom screen. When the Egg approaches 375°F (190°C) dome, about 10 minutes, slide the top of the daisy wheel partially closed, leaving it a quarter of the way open. When the Egg is up to temperature, remove the chicken from the marinade and place on the grate. Discard the marinade.

Grill the chicken until it reaches an internal temperature of 165°F (74°C), about 25 minutes. Remove from the Egg and set on a rack, tented with foil, for 10 minutes before serving.

CRISPY GRILLED CHICKEN

Crispy, moist, seasoned chicken is great when deep fried. This recipe replicates the same deep fried experience without actually deep frying. The buttermilk helps marinate the chicken, keeping it moist. The coating and spices give it the crispy and full-flavored taste you expect.

MAKES ABOUT 6 SERVINGS

3 lb (1.4 kg) chicken pieces

3 cups (720 ml) buttermilk

3 cups (362 g) crushed cornflakes or
1 cup (120 g) fresh bread crumbs

½ tsp sweet paprika

¼ tsp garlic powder

¼ tsp table salt

¼ tsp black pepper

¼ tsp cayenne pepper

Place chicken pieces and the buttermilk in a resealable plastic freezer bag or a casserole dish and refrigerate for 2 hours or overnight. In a medium bowl, mix together the remaining ingredients.

Set the Egg for 375°F (190°C) indirect with a drip pan. With the top and bottom vents wide open, light the fire and close the Egg. When the Egg gets up to about 250°F (121°C) dome, about 10 minutes, close the bottom screen. When the Egg approaches 375°F (190°C) dome, about 10 minutes, slide the top of the daisy wheel partially closed, leaving it a quarter of the way open. Remove the chicken from the buttermilk one at a time and place in the dry mixture bowl. Coat each chicken piece in the dry mixture and set aside for 10 to 15 minutes. When the Egg is up to temperature, place the coated chicken pieces on the Egg and grill until the internal temperature reaches 165°F (74°C), about 30 minutes. Let rest under tented aluminum foil on a rack for 5 minutes before serving.

POULTRY BALLS

These poultry balls can be made with either ground chicken or ground turkey.
They can be served on a toothpick or even in a lettuce wrap with shredded carrots and cucumber
and an Asian plum or duck sauce. Kids love them!

MAKES ABOUT 24 MEATBALLS

1 lb (454 g) 85% lean ground turkey or chicken

½ cup (30 g) fresh bread crumbs

¼ cup (38 g) finely chopped green onion, white and green portion

1 clove garlic, minced

1 tbsp (12 g) light brown sugar

1 tbsp (15 ml) soy sauce

1 large egg, lightly beaten

½ tsp kosher salt

Pinch black pepper

¼ cup (50 g) Basic Poultry Rub (see page 207)

In a large mixing bowl, mix all of the ingredients together. Mix thoroughly, but don't overhandle the meat, or it will make the meatballs less juicy. Gently roll the mixture into 1-inch (2.5-cm) meatballs and apply the rub.

Set the Egg for 350°F (180°C) indirect with a drip pan. With the top and bottom vents wide open, light the fire and close the Egg. When the Egg gets up to about 250°F (121°C) dome, about 10 minutes, close the bottom screen. When the Egg approaches 350°F (180°C) dome, about 10 minutes, slide the top of the daisy wheel partially closed, leaving it a quarter of the way open. Roast the meatballs, turning once halfway through for approximately 20 minutes, or to an internal temperature of 165°F (74°C). Serve with toothpicks as an appetizer.

TANDOORI CHICKEN

Tandoori Chicken traditionally is cooked in a tandoor, which is a wood-fired, clay bell-shaped oven originally found in India and Asia. The tandoor is a high heat source, and its recipes are well adapted to the Egg. The result is very moist chicken with a slightly spicy flavor, which balances with the creamy yogurt.

MAKES ABOUT 4 SERVINGS

MARINADE

1 cup (245 g) plain yogurt

2 tbsp (30 ml) vegetable oil

2 tsp (12 g) kosher salt

¼ tsp black pepper

2 tbsp (20 g) garlic, chopped

3 tbsp (30 g) ginger, chopped

2 tsp (10 g) ground coriander

1 tsp ground cumin

1 tsp ground turmeric

1 tsp garam masala

1 tsp paprika

½ tsp cayenne pepper

1 tsp lemon juice

3 lb (1.4 kg) cut-up chicken, bone in, skin on

To make the marinade, place all the ingredients, except the chicken, into a food processor or blender and mix until smooth, about 30 seconds. Reserve about ¼ cup (60 ml) of the marinade. Place the chicken and the blended marinade mixture into a resealable plastic freezer bag, massage well and refrigerate for 4 hours or overnight, massaging occasionally.

Set the Egg for 450°F (230°C) indirect with a drip pan. With the top and bottom vents wide open, light the fire and close the Egg. When the Egg gets up to about 250°F (121°C) dome, about 10 minutes, close the bottom screen. When the Egg approaches 450°F (230°C) dome, 10 to 15 minutes, slide the top of the daisy wheel partially closed, leaving it halfway open. Remove the chicken from the marinade and place skin-side down on the grate. Cook for about 15 minutes. Flip the chicken and brush with the reserved marinade and cook until the internal temperature reaches 165°F (74°C), about 15 more minutes. Let rest under tented aluminum foil on a rack for about 5 minutes.

INDIAN SPICED TURKEY BREAST

When you are expecting a large gathering, like at Thanksgiving, smoking a whole, fresh, all-natural turkey that you have brined yourself is the best way to go. However, when you just want moist, flavorful turkey breast, roasting a frozen, boneless, skin-on enhanced breast is very easy and good. Use a fresh, unenhanced boneless breast and brine it yourself, but trust me, you won't be sorry. In fact, while you are at it, why not make two?

MAKES ABOUT 8 SERVINGS

MARINADE PASTE

1 cup (240 ml) plain yogurt

½ cup (120 ml) lemon juice

2 tbsp (30 ml) olive oil

1 tbsp (15 ml) lemon zest

2 tsp (10 g) fresh ginger, minced

2 tsp (10 g) fresh garlic, minced

1 tsp hot paprika

½ tsp kosher salt

½ tsp ground cinnamon

½ tsp ground coriander

½ tsp ground cumin

½ tsp freshly ground black pepper

½ tsp cayenne pepper

3 lb (1.4 kg) fresh or frozen boneless turkey breast, injected with saline solution

In a medium bowl, mix all of the marinade ingredients together until well mixed. Rinse the turkey breast and pat dry. Add the marinade to the turkey on all of the meat, under the skin and on top of the skin. Refrigerate for 4 hours or overnight.

Set up the Egg for 350°F (180°C) indirect with a drip pan. With the top and bottom vents wide open, light the fire and close the Egg. When the Egg gets up to about 250°F (121°C) dome, about 10 minutes, close the bottom screen. When the Egg approaches 350°F (180°C) dome, about 10 minutes, slide the top of the daisy wheel partially closed, leaving it a quarter of the way open. Remove the turkey from the refrigerator and wipe off most of the marinade. Shape the breast into a small football shape, so all of the meat cooks more evenly. You do not need to tie it with butcher's twine. When the Egg is up to temperature, roast the turkey breast until the internal temperature reaches 165°F (74°C), about 60 minutes. When cooked, remove the breast and tent with aluminum foil on a rack for 10 minutes before slicing and serving.

LEMONGRASS CHICKEN

Lemongrass has a subtle citrus flavor and is not as pronounced as lemon juice. It is from Southeast Asia but can be found in most supermarkets. Use only the fresh, internal part. With the other herbs and spices, it creates a balanced flavor for the chicken. The lemongrass paste can also be used on lamb, veal and seafood.

MAKES ABOUT 6 SERVINGS

MARINADE PASTE

½ cup (10 g) lemongrass, chopped (If you can't find fresh lemongrass, lemongrass in tube form can be used as a substitution.)

1 tbsp (9 g) garlic, minced

2 tbsp (30 g) shallots, chopped

2 tbsp (5 g) cilantro, chopped

1 tbsp (15 g) ginger, chopped

1 tbsp (15 g) green chili (jalapeño), chopped

3 tbsp (36 g) brown sugar

1 tbsp (15 ml) fish sauce

1 tsp kosher salt

½ tsp ground black pepper

6 boneless, skinless chicken breasts

In a medium bowl, mix together all the ingredients, except the chicken. Make a paste out of the mixed marinade ingredients by using a mortar and pestle or a food processor. The paste may be made ahead of time and refrigerated.

Place the chicken and the marinade mixture in a resealable plastic freezer bag, massage well and refrigerate for 1 to 4 hours, massaging occasionally.

Set the Egg for 350°F (180°C) indirect with a drip pan. With the top and bottom vents wide open, light the fire and close the Egg. When the Egg gets up to about 250°F (121°C) dome, about 10 minutes, close the bottom screen. When the Egg approaches 350°F (180°C) dome, about 10 minutes, slide the top of the daisy wheel partially closed, leaving it a quarter of the way open. When the Egg is up to temperature, place the chicken on the Egg and grill, turning a few times, until the internal temperature reaches 165°F (74°C), about 15 minutes. Let rest under tented aluminum foil on a rack for about 5 minutes.

BOURBON MAPLE GLAZED SMOKED TURKEY

Cooking whole turkeys on the Egg has been quite commonplace for many Egg owners for several years now. Mad Max, a.k.a. Max Rosen, published his recipe back in the early 2000s and has had a "turkey hotline" before every Thanksgiving. Some people brine, some do not. I prefer brining because it promises a moist cook. You can stuff the bird with many different herbs, fruits and vegetables. If you are careful to make sure the pan juices don't burn you, you can make gravy from the delicious drippings. This recipe is not traditional Thanksgiving, but it doesn't need to be. The fowl is your canvas. Be as creative as you desire.

MAKES 8 TO 10 SERVINGS

BRINE

4 qt (3.8 L) cold water

1 cup (288 g) kosher salt

2 cups (475 ml) grade B maple syrup*

1 qt (950 ml) apple cider

1 qt (950 ml) peach nectar

1 cup (240 ml) bourbon

½ cup (120 ml) apple cider vinegar

1 tbsp (14 g) poultry seasoning

1 tbsp (6 g) black peppercorns, crushed

12 to 14 lb (5.4 to 6.3 kg) turkey

HERB BUTTER

2 tsp (10 g) fresh garlic, minced

1 stick (120 ml) unsalted butter, softened

Olive oil for roasting

Salt and pepper

FOR STUFFING BIRD

2 carrots, cut into 2-inch (5-cm) pieces

3 onions, each cut into 8 wedges

2 ribs of celery, cut into 2-inch (5-cm) pieces

1 apple, cored and cut into 8 wedges

4 sprigs fresh rosemary

BOURBON MAPLE GLAZE

½ cup (120 ml) maple syrup, grade B*

¼ cup (60 ml) bourbon

¼ cup (60 ml) honey

1 tbsp (15 ml) Dijon mustard

1 stick (120 ml) butter, melted

½ tsp cayenne pepper

Grade B maple syrup is preferred over grade A because it has more maple syrup flavor and is thicker.

(continued)

In an 8-quart (7.6-L) pot, bring 1 quart (950 ml) of water to a boil and add the salt to dissolve. Shut off the heat and stir in the maple syrup, and then all of the other brine ingredients. Refrigerate the brine for several hours to reduce the temperature to below 40°F (4°C).

Find a nonreactive container that is large enough to hold the turkey covered. If your refrigerator doesn't have enough room, you can use a food cooler and add ice around the turkey container.

When the brine has cooled, wash the turkey inside and out and remove all of the turkey accessories. Place the turkey into the brine container and add the cold brine. If there is not enough brine to cover the bird, add cold water. Brine the turkey, refrigerated for 12 to 24 hours.

Combine the garlic with the butter to make the herb butter. About an hour before cook time, remove the turkey from the brine and rinse completely, inside and out and pat dry. Discard the brine. Add the stuffing ingredients to the turkey. Place the turkey, breast-side up in a V rack in a roasting pan that will fit into the Egg. Rub the garlic butter under the breast skin, being gentle so as not to tear the skin. Rub the entire bird with olive oil and sprinkle generously with salt and pepper. Place a resealable plastic bag filled with ice on the breast. This will let the thigh meat cook to temperature at the same time as the breast. Remove the bag before cooking. Let the turkey come up to room temperature, about 1 hour before cooking.

Prepare the bourbon glaze in a medium saucepan. Heat the liquid ingredients to a simmer and reduce by half. Add the butter and the cayenne and simmer for 5 additional minutes to blend.

Set up the Egg for 350°F (180°C) indirect. With the top and bottom vents wide open, light the fire and close the Egg. When the Egg gets up to about 250°F (121°C) dome, about 10 minutes, close the bottom screen. When the Egg approaches 350°F (180°C) dome, about 10 minutes, slide the top of the daisy wheel partially closed, leaving it a quarter of the way open. When the Egg is up to temperature, place the roasting pan with the turkey on the grid. After about 1 hour, check the turkey to make sure the skin is not becoming too dark, and rotate the pan 180°. Check again after another hour and rotate the pan. If the skin is getting too dark, spritz it with some of the pan juices and tent it with foil. Check again in another hour. The total cook time should be about 4 hours, until the internal temperature of the breast is 165°F (74°C) and the thigh is 180°F (82°C). During the last 20 minutes of cooking, glaze the outside of the turkey with the maple bourbon glaze. Apply the glaze with a brush 2 or 3 times during the last 20 minutes until it is used up. When the turkey is cooked, tilt the cavity into the roasting pan to collect any juices for gravy. Set the turkey on a cooling rack, tented in foil, for 20 to 30 minutes to rest.

ASIAN INSPIRED CHICKEN WINGS

Chicken wings are my favorite white meat part of the chicken. If they are properly cooked,
I enjoy them grilled, smoked or deep fried. As with most Eggheads, I prefer dry wings over wet.
Too often the sauce covers up the crispy texture in the meat's surface.

MAKES ABOUT 8 SERVINGS

MARINADE

2 tbsp (20 g) garlic, minced

2 tbsp (25 g) brown sugar

2 tbsp (30 ml) dark soy sauce

3 tbsp (45 ml) oyster sauce

1 tbsp (15 ml) sriracha sauce

¼ cup (10 g) cilantro, chopped

½ tbsp (7.5 g) chili powder

¼ tsp ground black pepper

2 lb (900 g) whole chicken wings, tips removed

Mix all the marinade ingredients together in a medium bowl. Place the marinade in a resealable plastic freezer bag and add the wings. Massage the marinade around the chicken and lay the bag flat in a baking dish. Refrigerate for 4 to 12 hours, occasionally turning the bag.

Set the Egg for 350°F (180°C) indirect with a drip pan. With the top and bottom vents wide open, light the fire and close the Egg. When the Egg gets up to about 250°F (121°C) dome, about 10 minutes, close the bottom screen. When the Egg approaches 350°F (180°C) dome, about 10 minutes, slide the top of the daisy wheel partially closed, leaving it a quarter of the way open. Remove the wings from the marinade and discard the marinade. Rub the wings with your favorite chicken rub.

When the Egg is up to temperature, place the wings on the grid and grill until the internal temperature reaches 180°F (82°C), or about 25 minutes. Turn the wings every 5 minutes to prevent burning. When the wings are cooked, remove from the Egg and wait about 5 minutes before serving.

See photo on page 72.

ESPRESSO CHICKEN BREASTS

This recipe is for a dry marinade. The coffee introduces a deep, earthy flavor to the chicken that doesn't taste anything like coffee grounds. The coffee combines very well with the other spices and creates a distinctive flavor that will surprise you. Try it and you'll taste what I am saying!

MAKES 4 SERVINGS

ESPRESSO RUB

3 tbsp (17 g) freshly ground coffee

1 tbsp (18 g) kosher salt

1 tbsp (12 g) dark brown sugar

1 tsp ground black pepper

1 tsp garlic powder

1 tsp onion powder

4 boneless, skinless chicken breasts

2 tbsp (30 ml) olive oil

Salt

Pepper

In a medium bowl, mix all the rub ingredients together. Trim away any visible fat from the chicken breasts. Rub the chicken with olive oil, and apply the rub to each piece. Place the chicken in a resealable plastic freezer bag, and refrigerate for 4 hours or overnight.

Set the Egg for 350°F (180°C) indirect with a drip pan. With the top and bottom vents wide open, light the fire and close the Egg. When the Egg gets up to about 250°F (121°C) dome, about 10 minutes, close the bottom screen. When the Egg approaches 350°F (180°C) dome, about 10 minutes, slide the top of the daisy wheel partially closed, leaving it a quarter of the way open. Remove the chicken from the refrigerator and bring it up to room temperature, about 15 minutes. When the Egg is up to temperature, place the chicken on the grill, turning a few times, until the internal temperature of the chicken reaches 165°F (74°C), about 15 minutes. Let rest under tented aluminum foil on a rack for about 5 minutes before serving.

★ CHAPTER 4 ★

LOBSTER, SHRIMP, MAHI-MAHI & MORE FROM THE SEA'S BOTTOMLESS BOUNTY

We all know that fish and seafood are plentiful all over the world. The variety of available fish and seafood allows for many different flavorings and toppings that shine when grilled over charcoal. I used to be concerned with grilling fish because it is so delicate. Two things that help keep the fish intact are to make sure the grate is very clean and that it has been well oiled. Second, I use the double spatula method to turn fish. This method uses two spatulas, one in each hand. One goes under the fish and the other is propped up against it. Gently lean the fish over on to the second spatula, then lay the fish back down. For many, fish and seafood is a healthy choice. I eat it because it tastes good, especially off the grill!

SEA SCALLOPS WITH MANGO SALSA

When cooked correctly, scallops can be sweet, juicy and tender. They should not be overcooked, or they will be dry and chewy. Sea scallops are much larger than bay scallops and cost more. This recipe calls for sea scallops, but bay scallops can be substituted because we are not cooking on a grill grid grate, but in a pan. Scallops can be "wet" or "dry." Dry sea scallops taste much better than wet. Dry scallops are not treated. They are creamy and slightly pink in color. Wet scallops have been treated with preservatives and do not sear as well because they have retained liquid. Their color is very bright white. Frozen scallops are often frozen at sea and preservatives are not necessary. If the packaging doesn't say that no preservatives have been added, they may still be wet. Any fresh scallop should smell sweet and have an ocean smell, not a fishy smell.

MAKES ABOUT 4 SERVINGS

---

16 large, dry sea scallops

MARINADE

¼ cup (60 ml) soy sauce

1 tbsp (15 ml) Thai fish sauce

1 tbsp (15 ml) rice wine

2 tsp (10 ml) fresh garlic, minced

1 tsp fresh ginger, minced

1 tsp lime juice

5 small serrano peppers, seeded and minced

1 tbsp (15 ml) olive oil

Salt and pepper

Mango Salsa (page 98)

Rinse the scallops and remove the abductor muscle on the side. Mix all of the marinade ingredients together. Place scallops in the marinade and refrigerate for 30 minutes to 1 hour. Remove from the marinade, pat dry, coat with olive oil and sprinkle with salt and pepper.

Set the Egg for 350°F (180°C) direct and use either the half-round cast-iron griddle grate or a cast-iron frying-pan that fits in the Egg with a handle. With the top and bottom vents wide open, light the fire and close the Egg. When the Egg gets up to about 250°F (121°C) dome, about 10 minutes, close the bottom screen. When the Egg approaches 350°F (180°C) dome, about 10 minutes, slide the top of the daisy wheel partially closed, leaving it a quarter of the way open Add olive oil to coat the bottom of the griddle or pan and when hot, add the scallops. Sear for 2 to 3 minutes until browned, flip and cook for an additional 2 minutes. Cook until the inside is still soft and has a slightly opaque appearance. It should not be white. You can cook the first scallop and check for doneness before the others. They get chewy if they are overcooked. Serve the scallops with Mango Salsa.

MANGO SALSA

Fresh mango is the star of this salsa. It is sweet and also has a bit of spiciness to it.
The salsa goes well with grilled meats and fish. The ingredients can be changed to your preference.
You can try having more hot peppers, spices or even tomatoes. If the cucumbers are small,
you can wash them well and leave the skins on for more flavor and color.

MAKES ABOUT 4 CUPS (1.1 KG)

2 mangos, coarsely diced

1 cup (150 g) red onion, chopped

1 cup (150 g) cucumber, peeled and
chopped

⅓ cup (56 g) red bell pepper, chopped

¼ cup (10 g) fresh cilantro, chopped

2 tbsp (20 g) jalapeño pepper, seeded
and diced

2 tbsp (30 ml) lime juice

1 tbsp (12 g) brown sugar

2 tsp (10 g) fresh ginger, minced

1 tsp fresh garlic, minced

1 tsp kosher salt

½ tsp freshly ground black pepper

In a large bowl, mix all of the ingredients together. For best results, refrigerate for 2 hours before serving.

SALMON CAKES

Salmon cakes are easy to make and can be served by themselves or on a bun. This recipe uses fresh salmon. Others call for canned or leftover salmon, which is okay, but in this recipe the salmon is much sweeter and moister.

MAKES 6 SERVINGS

1½ lb (680 g) fresh salmon, skin removed, cut into 1-inch (2.5-cm) cubes

1 large egg, beaten

1 tbsp (15 ml) lemon juice

2 tbsp (30 ml) Dijon mustard

3 tbsp (45 ml) mayonnaise

½ tsp kosher salt

½ tsp garlic, minced

½ tsp freshly ground black pepper

¼ cup (10 g) fresh cilantro, chopped

¼ cup (10 g) fresh parsley, chopped

½ cup (75 g) bread crumbs

2 tbsp (30 ml) olive oil

6 toasted hamburger buns

Place the salmon, egg, lemon juice, mustard, mayonnaise, salt, garlic, pepper, cilantro and parsley in the bowl of a food processor and pulse about 4 or 5 times, keeping the salmon coarsely chopped. Place the bread crumbs in a medium bowl, then add the salmon mixture. Gently mix until well blended. Form into 6 patties.

Set the Egg for 350°F (180°C), direct, and use either the half-round cast-iron griddle grate or a cast-iron frying-pan that will fit on your Egg. With the top and bottom vents wide open, light the fire and close the Egg. When the Egg gets up to about 250°F (121°C) dome, about 10 minutes, close the bottom screen. When the Egg approaches 350°F (180°C) dome, about 10 minutes, slide the top of the daisy wheel partially closed, leaving it a quarter of the way open.

Add olive oil to coat the bottom of the griddle or pan and when hot, add the salmon cakes. Cook for 3 to 4 minutes per side—using the double spatula method, turning once—until golden brown. Remove from heat to a rack. Toast the hamburger rolls before adding the salmon patty. Serve with your choice of toppings, such as cole slaw or remoulade sauce.

The double spatula method for "flipping" food over is not really flipping but controlled turning. With a spatula in each hand, slide one under the meat while holding the other against the side of the meat to keep it from sliding. When the first spatula is under the meat, gently tip the meat onto the second spatula, and then remove the second spatula.

MAINELY LOBSTER

This recipe is a simple yet delicious way to eat Maine (North Atlantic) lobster. Growing up in New England, I am used to eating lobster, mostly boiled and dipped in drawn butter when cooked. Grilling over charcoal gives the lobster a subtle smoke flavor, delicious when basted with herb butter and cooked in its own juices. It's sweet, savory and a little smoky.

This recipe can also be used for spiny or rock lobsters from the Caribbean Sea, which don't have claws.

MAKES ABOUT 4 SERVINGS

---

4 (1½ lb [680 g]) fresh Maine lobsters

1 cup (240 ml) unsalted butter

2 tsp (6 g) garlic, finely minced

2 tbsp (5 g) parsley, chives or basil, finely chopped

1 tbsp (15 ml) lemon juice

Cut the live lobster in half, lengthwise. To do this, place the lobster on a rimmed cookie sheet on its belly with its head facing you. Using a heavy knife, press the point firmly down just behind the head and draw the knife toward you. The lobster will die instantly. Flip the lobster over with the tail toward you and slice it in half down the middle of the tail. Remove the green tamale and roe and discard. Crack the claws with the back side of the knife or with a mallet to break open the top side.

Melt the butter in a saucepan. Add garlic and all the spices, herbs, lemon juice and any juices from the cookie sheet and sauté for 3 to 4 minutes, until the garlic is softened.

Set the Egg for 400°F (200°C) indirect with a drip pan. With the top and bottom vents wide open, light the fire and close the Egg. When the Egg gets up to about 250°F (121°C) dome, about 10 minutes, close the bottom screen. When the Egg approaches 400°F (200°C) dome, about 10 minutes, slide the top of the daisy wheel partially closed, leaving it a quarter of the way open. When the Egg is up to temperature, place the lobster halves, shell-side down, and coat the flesh with the butter mixture. Add the mixture to the claws as well. Grill for approximately 10 minutes, or to an internal temperature of 145°F (63°C), basting with the butter mixture a couple of times when grilling. Place the remaining warm butter in 4 ramekins and serve with the lobster halves for dipping.

See photo on page 94.

GRILLED LEMON HONEY TILAPIA

Tilapia is a mild-flavored fish that is widely available due to fish farming. It's also reasonably priced. The lemon and honey add a sweet, citrus flavor that complements the fish. Serve on a plate with salsa or in freshly made Naan (page 169) or Pita Bread (page 164).

MAKES ABOUT 4 SERVINGS

LEMON HONEY BUTTER

2 tbsp (30 ml) honey

1 tsp lemon juice

4 oz (60 ml) unsalted butter

2 lb (900 g) tilapia

2 tbsp (30 ml) olive oil

1 tsp kosher salt

½ tsp freshly ground black pepper

In a small saucepan, blend the honey, lemon juice and butter together. Simmer until reduced by half, about 4 minutes. Let cool to room temperature.

Set up the Egg for 350°F (180°C) indirect with a drip pan. Make sure the grate is clean and well oiled. With the top and bottom vents wide open, light the fire and close the Egg. When the Egg gets up to about 250°F (121°C) dome, about 10 minutes, close the bottom screen. When the Egg approaches 350°F (180°C) dome, about 10 minutes, slide the top of the daisy wheel partially closed, leaving it a quarter of the way open. Rub the fish with olive oil and sprinkle with salt and pepper. When the Egg is up to temperature, grill the fish for about 4 minutes and brush the top side with the lemon honey butter glaze, flip using the double spatula method (page 99), glaze the top side and cook for another 3 minutes, until the internal temperature reaches about 135°F (57°C). When cooked, remove from the Egg and place under an aluminum foil tent on a rack to rest for 5 minutes.

CITRUS SHRIMP WITH CHIPOTLE

The marinade will add a little tartness to the shrimp in this recipe, and the chipotles
will add subtle, smoky heat. Grilled shrimp with just salt and pepper has good texture and flavor,
but the flavors in this marinade and baste greatly elevate the crisp shrimp.
Once you taste these, you might be sorry you didn't double the recipe.

MAKES ABOUT 8 SERVINGS

MARINADE

1 cup (240 ml) lemon juice

1 cup (240 ml) lime juice

1 cup (240 ml) orange juice

1 tbsp (10 g) garlic, minced

4 chopped canned chipotle peppers in
adobo sauce

2 tbsp (30 ml) olive oil

2 lb (900 g) raw shrimp, 16 to 20
count, peeled, deveined, with tails on

BASTE

½ cup (120 ml) unsalted butter,
melted

2 tbsp (5 g) fresh cilantro, finely
chopped

¼ tsp kosher salt

¼ tsp black pepper

2 tsp (10 ml) adobe sauce

Wisk all of the marinade ingredients in a medium bowl until well combined.
Place the marinade in a resealable plastic freezer bag and add the cleaned shrimp.
Refrigerate for 45 minutes, turning occasionally. With the amount of citrus in the
marinade, a longer marinate will make the shrimp mushy, so make sure to remove the
shrimp from the marinade after 45 minutes. For basting, melt the butter and add the
finely chopped cilantro, salt, pepper and adobo sauce.

Set the Egg for 350°F (180°C) indirect with a drip pan. With the top and bottom
vents wide open, light the fire and close the Egg. When the Egg gets up to about
250°F (121°C) dome, about 10 minutes, close the bottom screen. When the Egg
approaches 350°F (180°C) dome, about 10 minutes, slide the top of the daisy wheel
partially closed, leaving it a quarter of the way open. You may wish to add a second
grate on top of the first grate, turned 90 degrees so the shrimp won't fall through.
When the Egg is up to temperature, remove the shrimp from the marinade and place
on the grate, discarding the marinade.

Grill the shrimp for 3 minutes per side, basting often, until it is pink. Be careful not
to overcook! The shrimp should have a little give when pressed.

ADOBO HALIBUT WITH CORN, BLACK BEAN AND TOMATO SALSA

Halibut is a fairly firm white fish that will accept a marinade well. The adobo marinade is really a wet rub. The spices complement the acid of the citrus. With each bite, you will taste the sweetness of the fish, along with the garlic, cilantro and citrus juices. This is a very pleasant combination.

MAKES ABOUT 4 SERVINGS

ADOBO MARINADE

¾ cup (180 ml) lime juice

¾ cup (180 ml) orange juice

2 tbsp (30 ml) extra-virgin olive oil

2 tbsp (20 g) garlic, chopped

1 tbsp (2.5 g) fresh cilantro, chopped

1 tsp ground cumin

½ tsp kosher salt

½ tsp black pepper

½ tsp dried oregano

2 lb (900 g) halibut

2 tbsp (30 ml) olive oil

1 tsp kosher salt

½ tsp freshly ground black pepper

In a medium bowl, whisk all marinade ingredients together until they are well combined. Place the filets in a resealable plastic freezer bag with the marinade and refrigerate for 30 minutes to 1 hour.

Set up the Egg for 350°F (180°C) indirect with a drip pan. Make sure the grate is clean and well oiled. With the top and bottom vents wide open, light the fire and close the Egg. When the Egg gets up to about 250°F (121°C) dome, about 10 minutes, close the bottom screen. When the Egg approaches 350°F (180°C) dome, about 10 minutes, slide the top of the daisy wheel partially closed, leaving it a quarter of the way open Remove the fish from the marinade, pat dry, coat with olive oil and sprinkle with salt and pepper. When the Egg is up to temperature, grill the fish for about 4 minutes, flip using the double spatula method (page 99) and cook for another 3 minutes or until the internal temperature reaches about 135°F (57°C). When cooked, remove from the Egg and place under an aluminum foil tent on a rack to rest for 5 minutes. Serve with Corn, Tomato and Black Bean Salsa (page 106).

CORN, TOMATO AND BLACK BEAN SALSA

This salsa can be served with grilled meats, chicken, fish and seafood. Serve it on the side or include it in tacos, wraps or with tortilla chips. The fresh grilled corn gives it a great, smoky flavor. If you like it a little bit spicier, add additional jalapeño.

MAKES ABOUT 8 SERVINGS

2 ears fresh corn, shucked

1 tbsp (30 ml) olive oil

3 plum tomatoes, seeded and diced

1 cup (201 g) canned black beans, drained

¼ cup (40 g) red onion, chopped

¼ cup (60 ml) lime juice

⅓ cup (13 g) fresh cilantro, chopped

1 jalapeño pepper, seeded and finely chopped

1 green onion, chopped

½ tsp kosher salt

½ tsp freshly ground black pepper

Set the Egg for 350°F (180°C) indirect with a drip pan. With the top and bottom vents wide open, light the fire and close the Egg. When the Egg gets up to about 250°F (121°C) dome, about 10 minutes, close the bottom screen. When the Egg approaches 350°F (180°C) dome, about 10 minutes, slide the top of the daisy wheel partially closed, leaving it a quarter of the way open.

Coat the corn with olive oil. When the Egg is up to temperature, place the corn on the grid and cook for about 5 minutes, turning every minute. Be careful not to burn it. Remove the corn and set it on a rack, tented with foil, for 5 minutes.

When the corn is cool enough to handle, cut all of the kernels off of the ears and place them in a large bowl. After the kernels have been cut, take the back side of the knife blade and rub it down the ear, letting all the juice go into the bowl of kernels. When done with the corn, add all of the other ingredients to the bowl and mix well.

GARLIC BUTTER GRILLED OYSTERS

Many people eat oysters raw, straight from the shell. They like the sweetness and the liquor from the shell. This recipe cooks the oysters in their shells, retaining the sweet flavor and liquor, and also adds a "garlic butter bath." The grill adds just a little smoke.

MAKES ABOUT 4 SERVINGS

24 fresh oysters

GARLIC BUTTER TOPPING

6 tbsp (90 ml) unsalted butter, softened

3 tbsp (8 g) parsley, finely chopped

2 tbsp (6 g) chives, finely chopped

1 tbsp (15 g) fresh garlic, minced

1 tbsp (15 ml) lemon juice

2 tsp (1 g) dried rosemary

¼ tsp kosher salt

¼ tsp freshly ground black pepper

Rinse the oysters in cold water and scrub the shells. Throw away any oysters that remain open after scrubbing.

Set up the Egg for 500°F (260°C) direct. With the top and bottom vents wide open, light the fire and close the Egg. When the Egg gets up to about 250°F (121°C) dome, about 10 minutes, close the bottom screen. When the Egg approaches 500°F (260°C) dome, 10 to 15 minutes, slide the top of the daisy wheel partially closed, leaving it halfway open. Place all of the topping ingredients in a medium bowl and mix until the butter is evenly colored. When the Egg is up to temperature, burp it, being careful with flash back, and place the unopened oysters, round-side down, on the grate as level as possible. Cook the oysters for 3 or 4 minutes, until the oysters open. Remove from the Egg, and with a pair of tongs, pliers or ovenproof gloves, remove the top shell, being very careful not to spill any liquor from the bottom shell. Place 2 teaspoons (10 ml) of the garlic butter topping on each oyster. Discard any oysters that have not opened. Return the oysters to the Egg and cook with the topping on the oysters for another 2 to 3 minutes, until the internal temperature on the oyster is 145°F (63°C). Be careful not to overcook them. When cooked, remove from the Egg and serve.

MACADAMIA NUT CRUSTED MAHI MAHI

Mahi mahi is a firm-fleshed fish from the Pacific Ocean. When my wife and I took a cruise to Hawaii, we visited a macadamia orchard and declared macadamia nuts to be our new favorite. The crispy texture of the nut mixture complements the firmness of the fish. Serve the fish with Mango Salsa. This recipe can also be used with bass or haddock.

MAKES ABOUT 4 SERVINGS

CRUST

½ cup (60 g) macadamia nuts, crushed

½ cup (75 g) panko bread crumbs

2 tbsp (40 g) cornmeal

1 tsp kosher salt

½ tsp freshly ground black pepper

2 lb (900 g) mahi mahi

2 tbsp (30 ml) olive oil

Mango Salsa (see page 98)

To prepare the nut mixture, put all of the ingredients except the fish and olive oil into a food processor and pulse until finely chopped. Place the nut mixture onto a plate.

Cut the fish into 4 pieces. Rinse and pat them dry. Rub the pieces with olive oil and then coat each piece of fish with the nut mixture, pressing it into the flesh.

Set up the Egg for 350°F (180°C) indirect with a drip pan. Make sure the grate is clean and well oiled. With the top and bottom vents wide open, light the fire and close the Egg. When the Egg gets up to about 250°F (121°C) dome, about 10 minutes, close the bottom screen. When the Egg approaches 350°F (180°C) dome, about 10 minutes, slide the top of the daisy wheel partially closed, leaving it a quarter of the way open. When the Egg is up to temperature, grill the fish for about 5 minutes, flip using the double spatula method (page 99) and cook for another 4 minutes, until the internal temperature reaches about 135°F (57°C). When cooked, remove from the Egg and place under an aluminum foil tent on a rack to rest for 5 minutes. Serve with Mango Salsa.

GRILLED CLAMS CASINO

Clams casino was first introduced in the early 1900s in Rhode Island. There is some debate that they may have originated in Boston. You know how territorial New Englanders can be! The dish has long since been popular all over the country. At BBQ contests in New England, we often turn in "chef's choice." Chef's choice is a contest category in which the team can cook whatever it wants. There's a running joke started at the awards ceremony by Chris Hart of IQue and perpetuated by Mike Boisvert of Lakeside Smokers, when asked "Whudja cook?" the answer is always, "clams casino." New Englanders take credit for it even when we didn't cook it!

MAKES ABOUT 6 SERVINGS

---

2 slices applewood smoked bacon, chopped

½ cup (75 g) green bell pepper, stem, seeds and ribs removed, finely chopped

½ cup (75 g) shallots, minced

2 tbsp (18 g) garlic, minced

¼ cup (60 ml) unsalted butter

2 tbsp (30 ml) lemon juice

½ tsp kosher salt

½ tsp freshly ground black pepper

½ cup (75 g) seasoned Italian bread crumbs

24 littleneck or cherrystone clams

Dice the bacon, sauté in a saucepan until crisp and place in a large bowl. Fry the green pepper in the bacon fat until soft but not toasted. Put the pepper, shallots and garlic in the bacon bowl. Add the butter to the saucepan and melt. Once melted, add the butter and the bacon fat to the bacon bowl, along with the lemon juice, salt and pepper. Stir all the ingredients until well mixed, and then add the bread crumbs and combine thoroughly.

Set up the Egg for 500°F (260°C) direct. With the top and bottom vents wide open, light the fire and close the Egg. When the Egg gets up to about 250°F (121°C) dome, about 10 minutes, close the bottom screen. When the Egg approaches 500°F (260°C) dome, about 10 to 15 minutes, slide the top of the daisy wheel partially closed, leaving it halfway open.

Rinse the clams in cold water, and scrub the shells. Discard any clams that remain open after scrubbing. When the Egg is up to temperature, burp it being careful of flash back, and place the unopened clams, round-side down on the grate and cook for 5 to 8 minutes, until the clams open.

With a pair of tongs, pliers or ovenproof gloves, remove the top shell and place a dollop of bacon–bread crumb mixture on each clam. Discard any clams on the grate that have not opened. Continue to cook with the topping on the clams for another 3 or 4 minutes, until the internal temperature reaches about 150°F (65°C). Do not overcook. When cooked, remove from the Egg and serve.

SOUTH PACIFIC SHRIMP AND MANGO STIR-FRY

This shrimp has it all. With a short, hot stir-fry in a wok, you'll get tender shrimp, crisp snow peas, crunchy carrots and peppers, slightly spicy mango and a honey-garlic finish. And of course, salt pork cracklins!

MAKES ABOUT 8 SERVINGS

1 tbsp (15 g) cornstarch

¾ cup (180 ml) seafood broth or low-sodium chicken broth

2 tbsp (30 ml) honey

¼ lb (113 g) salt pork, diced into ¼-inch (6-mm) pieces, skin removed

1 tbsp (15 g) chopped garlic

½ cup (75 g) onions, diced

2 tbsp (30 ml) vegetable oil

1 cup (8 g) snow peas, stems and strings removed

1 cup (150 g) thinly sliced carrots

1 cup (150 g) red bell pepper, seeded, cut into ½-inch (13-mm) dice

1 cup (150 g) mango, peeled, cut into ½-inch (13-mm) dice

¼ tsp white pepper

2 lb (900 g) raw shrimp, peeled, deveined and tails off

In a medium bowl, combine the cornstarch, seafood broth and honey, and mix well.

Set the Egg for 450°F (230°C) dome direct. With the top and bottom vents wide open, light the fire and close the Egg. When the Egg gets up to about 250°F (121°C) dome, about 10 minutes, close the bottom screen. When the Egg approaches 350°F (180°C) dome, about 10 minutes, slide the top of the daisy wheel partially closed, leaving it halfway open. At 450°F (230°C) dome, burp the Egg, being careful with flash back, and place a wok on the Egg, sitting it on the fire ring and leaving the dome open. When a drop of water dances on the wok for a second or two, the wok is hot enough.

Add diced salt pork and brown it for about 1 minute. Add the garlic and the onion to the wok and stir-fry for 30 seconds, then remove from the wok. Add 2 tablespoons (30 ml) of oil, and when hot again, add the snow peas, carrots, peppers and mango and stir-fry for 3 minutes. Stir the white pepper into the seafood broth, then add the shrimp and stir-fry for another 2 minutes, until the shrimp is pale pink. Add the seafood broth mixture, cornstarch, garlic, onion and salt pork to the wok and stir-fry for 30 seconds. Continue to stir-fry until the shrimp is cooked through, or for about 2 more minutes.

CHAPTER 5

HANDHELDS, APPS & SELFIE STICKS

Some outdoor parties have a slow start and need grilled "teasers" to tide the guests over or just to tease them as to what's to come. The recipes in this chapter can be appetizers or served as the main course. Burgers, for instance, can be a main attraction or served as smaller-portion sliders. One kabob can be served as picky food or wrapped in naan or pita bread to make a satisfying sandwich. I really enjoy all of these recipes, but if I had to pick a personal favorite, it would be the Tequila Lime Turkey Nachos, Lamb Souvlaki with Tzatziki Cucumber Yogurt Dip, Sugarcane Shrimp and, yes, the Spam® Burger! Regardless of how or when, these grilled recipes always bring a grin and head nod.

CAJUN PORK AND SHRIMP BURGERS

Pork burgers are a great change from beef burgers and can be just as juicy.
Adding shrimp and Cajun spices makes these pork burgers unlike any beef burger.
This recipe uses a cast-iron griddle plate or frying pan to give the burger a crispy exterior.

MAKES ABOUT 5 SERVINGS

CAJUN SEASONING

2 tsp (4 g) sweet paprika

1 tsp kosher salt

1 tsp garlic powder

¾ tsp dried oregano

¾ tsp dried thyme

½ tsp onion powder

½ tsp freshly ground black pepper

½ tsp cayenne pepper

1 lb (450 g) ground pork, 80/20 blend

¼ lb (113 g) whole, uncooked shrimp, peeled, deveined and tails removed

3 scallions, white and green parts, diced

1 tbsp (15 ml) olive oil

5 toasted hamburger buns

Yellow mustard to taste

Set up the Egg for 350°F (180°C) direct with either the half-round cast-iron griddle pan or a cast-iron frying-pan that fits into the Egg. With the top and bottom vents wide open, light the fire and close the Egg. When the Egg gets up to about 250°F (121°C) dome, about 10 minutes, close the bottom screen. When the Egg approaches 350°F (180°C) dome, about 10 minutes, slide the top of the daisy wheel partially closed, leaving it a quarter of the way open. In a medium bowl, mix the Cajun seasoning ingredients together. Add the ground pork, shrimp and the green onion. Mix all together, being careful not to overwork the ground meat or it can be tough and less juicy. Use your finger tips and don't squeeze the meat between your fingers. Mix only until the spices are well dispersed. Form the burger mix into 5 patties, but do not overpack!

Add the olive oil to the griddle pan and swirl to cover. Place the burgers in the pan and cook for 3 minutes per side, until the internal temperature of the meat reaches at least 165°F (74°C). Remove the patties from the Egg and let rest on a rack for 5 minutes.

Place the sliced hamburger buns on the griddle and toast for 1 minute. Place the burgers on the bun with a squirt of yellow mustard before adding the top bun.

INDONESIAN COCONUT BEEF BURGERS

These burgers have a sweet and spicy flavor, which complements the beef very well.
The sweet and crunchy coconut blends with the heat from the peppers and other spices.
For an interesting condiment, serve it with Peanut Sauce (page 130).

MAKES ABOUT 8 SERVINGS

1 tsp ground cumin

1 tsp ground coriander

1 tsp kosher salt

½ tsp freshly ground black pepper

¼ tsp red pepper flakes

6 tbsp (90 g) shredded coconut

3 tbsp (7 g) fresh cilantro, chopped

2 tbsp (30 g) shallots, minced

½ tbsp (8 g) fresh ginger, minced

1 tsp garlic, minced

2 lb (900 g) ground chuck 80/20 mix

8 toasted hamburger buns

In a small bowl, combine all of the herbs and spices and mix well. In a large bowl, add the ground chuck and then the spices and mix until every ingredient is well dispersed. Take caution not to overwork or squeeze the meat because it can get tough and less juicy. Form the meat into 8 patties.

Set up the Egg for 400°F (200°C) dome, direct. With the top and bottom vents wide open, light the fire and close the Egg. When the Egg gets up to about 250°F (121°C) dome, about 10 minutes, close the bottom screen. When the Egg approaches 400°F (200°C) dome, about 10 to 12 minutes, slide the top of the daisy wheel partially closed, leaving it a quarter of the way open.

Place the burgers on the Egg with the dome open and cook for 4 minutes on the first side, flip and cook for 3 minutes on the second side. Remove from the heat and let rest for 5 minutes before serving.

THANKSGIVING TURKEY BURGERS

A lot of people use ground turkey or ground chicken for burgers. They can sometimes be a little bit dry. This recipe not only produces a juicy turkey burger but adds sweet potatoes, bread crumbs and spices reminiscent of a Thanksgiving turkey's. The cranberry sauce on top makes the holiday complete.

MAKES ABOUT 4 SERVINGS

¼ cup (40 g) bread crumbs

1 tsp poultry seasoning

½ cup (80 g) raw sweet potato, grated

2 tsp (2 g) fresh parsley, chopped

2 tsp (10 g) shallots, chopped

1 tsp kosher salt

½ tsp freshly ground black pepper

1 egg

1 lb (450 g) ground turkey

4 hamburger buns, toasted

4 tbsp (60 ml) whole cranberry sauce, divided

Mix all of the ingredients, except the buns and cranberry sauce, together in a bowl. Form the burger mix into 4 patties, gently using the palms of your hands, but do not squeeze them tightly. They should hold together on their own, but don't press them too hard.

Set up the Egg for 400°F (200°C) indirect. With the top and bottom vents wide open, light the fire and close the Egg. When the Egg gets up to about 250°F (121°C) dome, about 10 minutes, close the bottom screen. When the Egg approaches 400°F (200°C) dome, about 10 to 12 minutes, slide the top of the daisy wheel partially closed, leaving it a quarter of the way open. Place the burgers on the Egg and cook for 4 minutes on the first side, flip and cook for 3 minutes on the second side, until the internal temperature reaches 165°F (74°C). Remove from the heat and let rest for 5 minutes. Serve on a toasted bun with 1 tablespoon (15 ml) cranberry sauce on top.

SPAM® BURGERS

I grew up eating Spam® (which is a cooked, canned block of chopped pork shoulder and ham).
My kids didn't and their kids don't. There are two generations that think Spam® is something
manufactured, undesired and of suspicious origin. Maybe the definition sticks, but the Spam®
I know tastes great, regardless of where it came from! Growing up, we often had Spam® sandwiches
for school or fried Spam® with eggs. Spam® helped the United States get through World War II and is
now very popular in Hawaii and with all those who remember. This burger is no joke.
It brings back the flavors of my childhood. Try it. I know you will enjoy it.

MAKES ABOUT 4 SERVINGS

2 (12 oz [340 g]) cans Spam®

1 large egg, beaten

¼ cup (60 g) onion, minced

¼ cup (60 g) green bell pepper, minced

¼ cup (30 g) panko bread crumbs

1 tbsp (15 ml) prepared yellow mustard

¼ tsp kosher salt

1 tsp freshly ground black pepper

1 tbsp (15 ml) olive oil

4 (¼-inch [6-mm]) slices of Velveeta®

4 slices canned pineapple

2 tbsp (30 ml) honey

Pinch ground cinnamon

Pinch ground nutmeg

4 toasted hamburger buns

Put the Spam® through a meat grinder or mince it in a food processor. In a large bowl, combine the egg, onion, green pepper, panko, mustard, salt and black pepper. Mix well and form the mixture into 4 patties.

Set up the Egg for 350°F (180°C) direct with either the half-round cast-iron griddle-pan or a cast-iron frying-pan that fits into the Egg. With the top and bottom vents wide open, light the fire and close the Egg. When the Egg gets up to about 250°F (121°C) dome, about 10 minutes, close the bottom screen. When the Egg approaches 350°F (180°C) dome, about 10 minutes, slide the top of the daisy wheel partially closed, leaving it a quarter of the way open.

Add the olive oil to the griddle pan and swirl to cover. Place the burgers in the pan and cook for 3 minutes, then flip and continue to cook until the internal temperature of the meat reaches at least 165°F (74°C). After the first flip, add the Velveeta® to the top of the burger. Remove the patties from the Egg and let rest on a rack for 5 minutes.

While the burgers are resting, add the pineapple slices to the griddle pan and sear on the Egg for 1½ minutes, then flip. Add the honey and spices to the top of the pineapple and continue to grill for 1 minute more. Place the sliced hamburger buns on the griddle and toast for 1 minute. Place the pineapple slice on the bottom bun, top with the burger and then the top bun.

TEQUILA LIME TURKEY NACHOS

Did I have you at tequila? Turkey thighs are the juiciest part of the bird, and when cooked to 165°F (74°C), they are also tender and tasty. The tequila marinade imparts a slightly spicy, fruity, sweet and earthy flavor to the thighs that will make you want more, bite after bite.

MAKES ABOUT 8 SERVINGS

MARINADE

¼ cup (60 ml) good quality tequila, 100% agave

2 tbsp (18 g) garlic, minced

1 jalapeño pepper, diced

2 tbsp (30 ml) lime juice

¼ cup (60 ml) orange juice

½ tsp salt

½ tsp black pepper

1 tbsp (2.5 g) fresh cilantro, finely chopped

1 tbsp (12 ml) olive oil

3 turkey thighs, bone-in, skinless, about 3 lb (1.4 kg)

TOPPINGS

2 poblano peppers, cut in half lengthwise, seeded, ribs and stems removed

1 large onion, sliced crosswise, about ⅜-inch (9-mm) thick

1 medium red bell pepper, cut in half lengthwise, stem removed

1 large tomato, sliced crosswise into about ⅜-inch (9-mm) thick slices

3 tbsp (45 ml) olive oil

1 tbsp (18 g) kosher salt

1 tbsp (7 g) freshly ground black pepper

Shredded cheese

CHIPS

8 flour tortillas, cut into 8 triangles each

3 cups (720 ml) vegetable oil for frying

Whisk all marinade ingredients in a medium-sized bowl and combine well. Place the marinade in a resealable plastic freezer bag and add the skinless thighs. Massage the marinade around the thighs and lay bag flat in a baking dish. Refrigerate for 4 to 6 hours, turning occasionally.

Set the Egg for 350°F (180°C) indirect with a drip pan. With the top and bottom vents wide open, light the fire and close the Egg. When the Egg gets up to about 250°F (121°C) dome, about 10 minutes, close the bottom screen. When the Egg approaches 350°F (180°C) dome, about 10 minutes, slide the top of the daisy wheel partially closed, leaving it a quarter of the way open. Remove the turkey from the marinade and place on the grate. Discard the marinade.

(continued)

When the Egg is up to temperature, grill the thighs until they reach an internal temperature of 180°F (82°C), about 45 minutes. Remove from the Egg and set on a rack, tented with aluminum foil, for 10 minutes before shredding.

While the turkey is roasting, prepare the toppings. Rub the toppings with olive oil and sprinkle with salt and pepper. Grill the toppings on the outside edge of the grate, away from the turkey and drip pan for 10 to 15 minutes, until slightly charred, turning as needed to prevent burning. When cooked, coarsely chop the toppings. Add them to a medium bowl with the lime juice and half of the cilantro.

When the turkey is cooked, add the vegetable oil to the Dutch oven, away from the Egg and cover. Place it on the Egg and heat the oil to a temperature of 350°F (180°C), about 15 minutes. When the oil is hot enough, keep the lid of the Egg open and fry the tortilla pieces until crispy, about 1 minute. Remove from the oil and place on a rack to cool. Finish cooking the tortillas. Place the cover back on the Dutch oven before removing it from the Egg and placing it in a safe place to cool off.

On a large cookie sheet or pizza pan, place a layer of chips on the bottom. Place the shredded turkey over the chips, and sprinkle the topping mix over the turkey. Sprinkle the shredded cheese on top and place back on the Egg with the dome closed, until the cheese melts, about 5 minutes. When the cheese is melted, sprinkle with salt and pepper and the rest of the chopped cilantro and serve.

MEAT OLIVES

Meat olives are steak rolls stuffed with a bacon, mushroom, onion, herb and spicey mixture. They are popular in Scotland and the Mediterranean. The stuffing is moist and flavorful. You can try adding additional ingredients such as cheese or cooked sausage.

MAKES ABOUT 6 SERVINGS

STUFFING

3 slices bacon, chopped

¼ cup (40 g) mushrooms, chopped

1 medium onion, chopped

1 tsp garlic, minced

½ tsp kosher salt

¼ tsp freshly ground black pepper

1 cup (60 g) bread crumbs

1 tsp fresh thyme

1 tbsp (2.5 g) fresh parsley, chopped

4 top round steaks, about 1-inch (2.5-cm) thick

2 tbsp (30 ml) prepared whole-grain mustard

Butcher's twine

Olive oil

1 tsp kosher salt

½ tbsp (3 g) freshly ground black pepper

To prepare the stuffing, over medium heat, cook the bacon in a pan until partially crisp, about 5 minutes. Remove the bacon to a medium bowl. In the bacon fat, sauté the mushrooms and onion until the onion is translucent but not crisp, about 5 minutes. Place the vegetables in the bowl with the bacon. Add the garlic to the pan and sauté until softened, but not browned, and add to the mushrooms, onions and bacon. Add the remaining stuffing ingredients to the bowl and mix well. If the stuffing is dry, add some of the bacon fat to moisten.

The steak needs to be made thinner and pounded flat. Place the steak on a cutting board. Using a sharp knife, slice through the steak to make it half its thickness. Place a piece of plastic wrap over the top of the thinner steaks and pound them with a mallet until they are about ¼ inch (6 mm) thick.

When all of the steaks are flattened, spread them with the mustard to coat the top side. Divide the stuffing between all of the steaks and roll each of them up around the stuffing. Fold the ends of the steaks into the roll and tie them with butcher twine, about every 1 inch (2.5 cm).

Spread the olive oil on the outside of the rolls and sprinkle them with salt and pepper.

Set the Egg for high heat, 350°F (180°C), direct. With the top and bottom vents wide open, light the fire and close the Egg. When the Egg gets up to about 250°F (121°C) dome, about 10 minutes, close the bottom screen. When the Egg approaches 350°F (180°C) dome, about 10 minutes, slide the top of the daisy wheel partially closed, leaving it a quarter of the way open.

Place the meat on the Egg for about 12 minutes, turning every 3 minutes. Continue cooking until the internal temperature reaches 135°F (57°C). Remove, cover with foil and let the meat rest for 5 to 10 minutes. The internal temperature should rise to 145°F (63°C). Cut into ½-inch (1.5-cm) slices and serve.

INDONESIAN BEEF SATAY

Satay is a big street food in Indonesia and Southern Asia. Meat is marinated, then skewered and cooked over high heat. Like all things cooked on the Egg, the flavors are great and the subtle smoke accents the meat very well. This recipe is for beef satay with Peanut Dipping Sauce.

MAKES ABOUT 6 SERVINGS

1 cup (240 ml) coconut milk

3 tbsp (45 g) shallots, minced

2 tbsp (30 ml) fish sauce

2 tbsp (23 g) light brown sugar

1 tbsp (15 ml) Sriracha sauce

1 tbsp (15 ml) lime juice

1 tbsp (15 ml) sesame oil

1 tbsp (9 g) garlic, minced

½ tbsp (7 g) fresh ginger, minced

1 tsp kosher salt

1 tsp ground coriander

1 tsp ground cumin

½ tsp ground turmeric

½ tsp freshly ground black pepper

2 lb (900 g) flank steak

20 (8-inch [20-cm]) wooden skewers, presoaked

Peanut Dipping Sauce (page 130)

Cucumber Salad (page 149)

Combine all ingredients except the meat, mixing well, and place in a doubled-up 1-gallon (3.8-L) freezer bag, removing as much air as possible, and seal. Cut the flank steak into 3-inch (7.6-cm) wide pieces with the grain, then slice each piece against the grain in a diagonal cut, yielding ¼-inch (6-mm) thick pieces. Add the sliced beef to the marinade and place in the refrigerator for at least 4 hours or overnight. Flip the bag often, massaging the marinade into the meat.

Set the Egg for 450°F (230°C) direct. With the top and bottom vents wide open, light the fire and close the Egg. When the Egg gets up to about 250°F (121°C) dome, about 10 minutes, close the bottom screen. When the Egg approaches 450°F (230°C) dome, about 10 to 15 minutes, slide the top of the daisy wheel partially closed, leaving it halfway open. Take the meat out of the bag and discard the marinade. Thread the strips of beef onto the presoaked skewers, leaving a couple of inches on the blunt end for a handle.

Place the skewered meat on an oiled grid and cook about 2 minutes per side, to an internal temperature of 165°F (74°C), about 4 minutes total, being careful to turn the skewers often to keep the sugars in the marinade from burning. Serve beef satay with Peanut Dipping Sauce (page 130) and Cucumber Salad (page 149).

CHICKEN SATAY

Use the same marinade and cooking instructions as for Beef Satay. My preference is to use 2 pounds (900 g) of boneless chicken thighs. Trim them of any silver skin or fatty pieces. Cut them into ¼-inch (6-mm) slices.

Serve with Peanut Dipping Sauce.

PORK SATAY

Use the same marinade and cooking instructions as for Beef Satay. My preference is to use trimmed slices of pork butt, cut into ¼-inch (6-mm) slices. You can use a pork butt, or buy Country Style ribs from the butt (not the loin) for slicing.

Serve with Peanut Dipping Sauce.

PEANUT DIPPING SAUCE

MAKES 4 SERVINGS

⅔ cup (119 g) creamy peanut butter, unsalted and unsweetened, if available

¼ cup (60 ml) canned unsweetened coconut milk, stirred well

¼ cup (60 g) shallots, minced

3 tbsp (45 ml) fish sauce

1 tbsp (15 ml) lime juice

4 tsp (13 g) fresh garlic, minced

1 tsp red chili paste

⅓ cup (80 ml) warm water, if needed

¼ cup (10 g) fresh cilantro, chopped

In a medium bowl, blend all of the ingredients together except for the water and cilantro. The mixture should not be thick or extremely runny. Add some of the warm water to thin out the mix if required. If too runny, add more peanut butter and remix. Serve at room temperature with fresh cilantro on top.

TZATZIKI, GREEK CUCUMBER YOGURT DIP

This is a cool and refreshing dipping sauce that goes well with lamb kabobs. It also makes a nice dipping sauce for vegetables and is commonly used in sandwiches and gyros or on Greek salad. The dip should be made and refrigerated for 2 hours before serving, to blend the flavors.

MAKES ABOUT 2 CUPS (473 ML)

½ cup (75 g) cucumber, seeded and diced

½ tsp kosher salt

2 tsp (6 g) fresh garlic, minced

1 tbsp (15 ml) lemon juice

1 tbsp (5 g) fresh dill, chopped

Freshly ground black pepper

2 cups (480 ml) Greek yogurt, strained

Put cucumber in a colander, sprinkle with salt and let stand for 30 minutes to draw out water. Drain well and wipe dry with paper towel.

In a food processor with steel blade, add cucumber, garlic, lemon juice, dill and a few grinds of black pepper. Process this mixture until well blended, then stir it into the yogurt. Taste before adding any extra salt, and then salt if needed.

This will keep for a few days in the refrigerator, but you will need to drain off any water and stir each time you use it.

LAMB SOUVLAKI

Lamb souvlaki is a Greek marinated lamb kabob, grilled on skewers. The lamb is very tender and the distinct flavors of the marinade match well to the distinct flavor of the lamb. Serve with Tzatziki (page 131) and Pita Bread (page 164) for a great snack.

MAKES ABOUT 10 SERVINGS

MARINADE

½ cup (120 ml) olive oil

2 tbsp (30 ml) lemon juice

¼ cup (40 g) red onion, finely chopped

2 tsp (6 g) fresh garlic, minced

1 tsp dried thyme

1 tsp dried oregano

½ tsp kosher salt

¼ tsp freshly ground black pepper

3 lb (1.4 kg) boneless lamb leg or shoulder

20 (8-inch [20-cm]) long wooden skewers, presoaked

Combine all of the marinade ingredients and place in a doubled-up 1-gallon (3.8-L) freezer bag. Remove any visible fat or silver skin from the lamb. Cut the lamb into 1½-inch (4-cm) square pieces.

Place the meat in the plastic bag, removing as much air as possible, and seal. Marinate in the refrigerator for 2 to 4 hours, turning and massaging the bag a few times.

Set the Egg up for 400°F (200°C) direct. With the top and bottom vents wide open, light the fire and close the Egg. When the Egg gets up to about 250°F (121°C) dome, about 10 minutes, close the bottom screen. When the Egg approaches 400°F (200°C) dome, about 10 to 12 minutes, slide the top of the daisy wheel partially closed, leaving it a quarter of the way open. Take the lamb out of the bag, reserving the marinade, and place the pieces on presoaked skewers. Leave space on the blunt end of the skewer for a handle. Place the skewers on an oiled grid and cook to an internal temperature of at least 165°F (74°C), about 8 minutes, turning every minute to make sure the sugar in the marinade doesn't burn. A little char is good.

Boil the marinade for 5 minutes and use it to mop the skewers. Use it as a dipping sauce by boiling it again for 5 minutes after the final mop and before serving.

SUGARCANE SHRIMP

This shrimp on a sugarcane stick is a real treat. The shrimp itself is sweet with a little spice, and when you are done eating the shrimp, you can chew and suck on the sugarcane! Sugarcane is available online, in Asian markets and in some supermarkets. Ask the produce manager for it. It's worth it!

MAKES ABOUT 4 SERVINGS

1 lb (450 g) raw shrimp, peeled, deveined and tail off, dried then chopped

¼ cup (40 g) shallots, chopped

2 tbsp (20 g) jalapeño pepper, seeded and ribbed, chopped

1 tbsp (15 ml) fish sauce

2 tsp (20 g) turbinado sugar

1 egg, beaten

½ tbsp (5g) garlic, minced

½ tsp kosher salt

Pinch of freshly ground black pepper

1 tbsp (15 ml) vegetable oil

1 piece sugarcane, 8-inch (20-cm) long

Combine all of the ingredients except the oil and sugarcane in a food processor and pulse until minced into a paste. Refrigerate for at least 30 minutes.

Remove the outer bark of the sugarcane. Stand it upright on a cutting board and split it down the middle. Continue to split the sugarcane until it is in 8 similar-sized pieces.

Set up the Egg for 400°F (200°C) direct. With the top and bottom vents wide open, light the fire and close the Egg. When the Egg gets up to about 250°F (121°C) dome, about 10 minutes, close the bottom screen. When the Egg approaches 400°F (200°C) dome, about 10 to 12 minutes, slide the top of the daisy wheel partially closed, leaving it a quarter of the way open.

Take the shrimp paste out of the refrigerator and pack 2 tablespoons (30 ml) of paste onto the upper half of the sugarcane skewer. Place the filled skewer on a plate with the vegetable oil and roll the shrimp until it is coated. Repeat until all of the skewers are made.

Place the shrimp on an oiled grid and cook, turning every minute to an internal temperature of at least 160°F (71°C), about 4 to 5 minutes total. Remove to a plate and serve.

CARIBBEAN CHICKEN, BACON AND MANGO KABOBS

So, we have all the Caribbean warm breezes, rum, mangos and bacon! Why not grill some chicken kabobs? These are good for an appetizer, main course or even a snack. If you like them spicier, add a little cayenne pepper to the marinade. Do you like them sweeter? Add some molasses to the glaze at the end. Sit back and enjoy yourself!

MAKES ABOUT 8 TO 10 SERVINGS

MARINADE

¼ cup (60 ml) dark rum

2 tbsp (20 g) jalapeño pepper, seeded and ribs removed, diced

2 tbsp (30 ml) lime juice

2 tbsp (62 g) turbinado sugar

1 tsp cinnamon, ground

1 tsp nutmeg, ground

½ tsp kosher salt

½ tsp freshly ground black pepper

2 lb (900 g) boneless chicken breasts, cut into 1-inch (2.5-cm) cubes

2 firm bananas

6 thin bacon slices

16 (8-inch [20-cm]) long wooden skewers, presoaked

2 mangos

2 tbsp (30 ml) unsalted butter

In a medium bowl, combine all of the marinade ingredients. Mix well and place in a doubled-up 1-gallon (3.8-L) freezer bag. Remove any visible fat from the chicken and cut chicken into 1-inch (2.5-cm) square pieces. Place the trimmed chicken in the plastic bag, removing as much air as possible, and seal. Marinate in the refrigerator for 2 to 4 hours, turning and massaging the bag a few times.

Set the Egg up for 400°F (200°C) direct. With the top and bottom vents wide open, light the fire and close the Egg. When the Egg gets up to about 250°F (121°C) dome, about 10 minutes, close the bottom screen. When the Egg approaches 400°F (200°C) dome, about 10 to 12 minutes, slide the top of the daisy wheel partially closed, leaving it a quarter of the way open.

Peel and cut the bananas into 1-inch (2.5-cm) pieces. Cut the bacon slices into 4-inch (10-cm) strips and wrap them around each banana slice. When it is time to skewer the bananas, run the presoaked skewer sideways through the outside of the banana. Slice the mango into ¾-inch (19-mm) slices, remove the skin and cut the mangos into ¾-inch (19-mm) cubes.

Take the chicken out of the bag, reserving the marinade, and place the chicken pieces on skewers, alternating with the mangos and bananas. Leave space on the blunt end of the skewer for a handle. Sprinkle each skewer with salt and pepper.

Place the skewers on an oiled grid and cook to an internal temperature of at least 165°F (74°C), about 8 minutes, turning every 2 minutes. Boil the reserved marinade and the butter together for 5 minutes and use it to mop the skewers when cooled.

COLOMBIAN BEEF KABOBS

South America is well known as a great beef continent. Beef kabobs are common street food. The blade steak is a great cut to use. It takes the marinade well and is very tender and flavorful. If you wish, you can add some 1-inch (2.5-cm) square pieces of bell pepper or red onion to the skewers.

MAKES ABOUT 6 SERVINGS

MARINADE

½ cup (120 ml) dark beer

2 tbsp (30 ml) lime juice

2 tbsp (30 ml) vegetable oil

¼ cup (40 g) red onion, minced

¼ cup (12 g) green onion, chopped

2 tsp (6 g) fresh garlic, minced

1 tsp dried cumin

½ tsp kosher salt

½ tsp freshly ground black pepper

2 lb (900 g) blade or sirloin steak

16 (8-inch [20-cm]) wooden skewers, presoaked

Combine all of the ingredients except the steak. Mix well and place in a doubled-up 1-gallon (3.8-L) freezer bag. Remove any visible fat and the center gristle from the blade steak. Cut the steak into 1-inch (2.5-cm) square pieces.

Once trimmed and sliced, place the steak in the plastic bag, removing as much air as possible, and seal the bag. Marinate in the refrigerator for at least 4 hours, or overnight, turning and massaging the bag a few times.

Set the Egg up for 400°F (200°C) direct. With the top and bottom vents wide open, light the fire and close the Egg. When the Egg gets up to about 250°F (121°C) dome, about 10 minutes, close the bottom screen. When the Egg approaches 400°F (200°C) dome, about 10 to 12 minutes, slide the top of the daisy wheel partially closed, leaving it a quarter of the way open. Take the steak out of the bag and thread it onto the skewers. Leave space on the blunt end of the skewer for a handle. Place the steak onto an oiled grid and cook to an internal temperature of at least 145°F (63°C), about 2 minutes per side and 8 minutes total. Serve the skewers on a platter with a cold beer.

CHICKEN YAKITORI

I prefer to use boneless chicken thighs because they are juicier than breasts. You can also use boneless turkey thighs. You can buy premade yakitori marinade, but homemade yakitori sauce is far better than store-bought. This recipe tastes fresher and brighter than sauce from a bottle. Serve as an appetizer or with white rice.

MAKES ABOUT 6 SERVINGS

1 cup (240 ml) light soy sauce

⅓ cup (80 ml) sake or dry sherry

2 tbsp (30 ml) honey

1 tbsp (9 g) garlic, chopped

2 tbsp (30 g) ginger, grated or chopped

2 lb (900 g) boneless chicken thighs

3 colored bell peppers, red, yellow and green, stems and ribs removed, seeded and cut into 2-inch (5-cm) squares

12 (1-inch [2.5-cm]) mushrooms, halved

20 (8-inch [20-cm]) wooden skewers, presoaked

Combine all of the ingredients except the chicken, peppers and mushrooms. Mix well and place in a doubled-up 1-gallon (3.8-L) freezer bag. Remove any visible fat or silver skin from the chicken. Cut the chicken into 1½-inch (4-cm) square pieces.

Once trimmed and sliced, place the chicken in the plastic bag, removing as much air as possible, and seal. Marinate in the refrigerator for 2 to 4 hours, turning and massaging the bag a few times.

Set the Egg up for 400°F (200°C) direct. With the top and bottom vents wide open, light the fire and close the Egg. When the Egg gets up to about 250°F (121°C) dome, about 10 minutes, close the bottom screen. When the Egg approaches 400°F (200°C) dome, about 10 to 12 minutes, slide the top of the daisy wheel partially closed, leaving it a quarter of the way open. Take the chicken out of the bag, reserving the marinade, and place the chicken pieces on skewers, alternating the chicken pieces with the vegetables on the skewers. Leave space on the blunt end of the skewer for a handle. Place the chicken on an oiled grid and cook to an internal temperature of at least 165°F (74°C), about 8 minutes. Turn every 2 minutes to make sure the sugar in the marinade doesn't burn. A little char is good.

Boil the marinade for 5 minutes and use it to mop the skewers. If serving it as a dipping sauce, boil it again for 5 minutes after the final mop and before serving.

QUESADILLAS

Quesadillas are akin to a Mexican grilled cheese sandwich. When grilled with a fresh tortilla, they are crunchy, creamy and have a subtle smoky flavor. This recipe is very basic. You can add any number of cooked ingredients, such as grilled vegetables, shredded chicken or pork or crumbled sausage.

MAKES ABOUT 6 SERVINGS

12 (6-inch [15-cm]) Corn Tortillas (page 167)

2 tbsp (30 ml) olive oil

1 cup (130 g) shredded pepper jack cheese

1 cup (130 g) shredded sharp cheddar cheese

½ cup (25 g) green onion, chopped

¼ cup (40 g) pickled jalapeños, diced

The quesadilla can be grilled two different ways. One is to lightly oil the outside of 1 tortilla, add ½ of the ingredients on half and fold it over to grill. The other way is to oil and lay 1 tortilla down and spread ⅙ of the topping over the whole surface, then place a second tortilla on top. Lightly oil the outside of the tortilla before grilling.

Set up the Egg for 350°F (180°C) direct. With the top and bottom vents wide open, light the fire and close the Egg. When the dome temperature gets up to about 250°F (121°C), about 10 minutes, close the bottom screen. When the dome temperature approaches 350°F (180°C), about 5 to 10 minutes, slide the top of the daisy wheel partially closed, leaving it a quarter of the way open.

When the Egg is up to temperature, grill the quesadillas on a raised grate for about 2 minutes per side, flipping once. Be careful not to burn them. When grilled, let the quesadillas rest for a couple of minutes before slicing into quarters.

★ **CHAPTER 6** ★

ACCOMPLICES, SLAWS, SALADS, SAUCES & VEGGIES

When I was growing up with my five siblings, we often heard, "Eat your vegetables!" The "suggestion" was never directed at me. I love vegetables, especially corn, beets and Brussels sprouts. We had a large garden and during the summer I was on maintenance duty. I remember that when I was about five years old, my neighbor took me into his garden, picked a ripe tomato and handed it to me. He told me to smell it and to eat it. I don't remember much from when I was five, but I certainly remember that a tomato doesn't smell or taste any better than when freshly picked. However, most of the vegetables I ate, although tasty, were boiled or steamed. I have learned that grilling them not only maintains flavors lost in boiling but also adds a crispiness and a slightly smoky flavor.

POBLANOS RELLENOS DE QUESO

These chilies have great flavor and texture and are not too hot. The crunchy batter yields to the sweet pepper and creamy, cheesy stuffing. You can create your own stuffing by adding cooked, diced bacon or pork, sausage or shredded chicken. Served with salsa on the side, this makes a great snack or side dish.

MAKES ABOUT 6 SERVINGS

6 whole poblano peppers

½ cup (45 g) sharp cheddar cheese, shredded

½ cup (45 g) Monterey jack cheese, shredded

1 cup (90 g) cream cheese, cut into ½ inch (12 mm) cubes

1 tbsp (2.5 g) cilantro, freshly chopped

1 tbsp (2.5 g) chives, chopped

1 tbsp (6.2 g) pork rub

1 cup (120 g) all-purpose flour

2 large eggs, well beaten

1 cup (160 g) stone-ground cornmeal

1 qt (950 ml) vegetable oil for frying

Slice each poblano along one side, from end to end, keeping the stem intact. Grill on direct heat over flames, on the Egg or over a gas burner, turning often until the skin is charred and blistering. Place the grilled poblano into a resealable plastic bag for about 20 minutes to steam.

While the poblanos are steaming, mix all of the cheeses, herbs and spices together in a large bowl. When the peppers have steamed, remove from the bag and peel the skins off. Carefully remove the ribs and seeds. Spoon the cheese mixture into the peppers, reshape and refrigerate for about an hour.

Set the Egg for 400°F (200°C) direct. With the top and bottom vents wide open, light the fire and close the Egg. When the Egg gets up to about 250°F (121°C) dome, about 10 minutes, close the bottom screen. When the Egg approaches 400°F (200°C) dome, about 10 to 12 minutes, slide the top of the daisy wheel partially closed, leaving it a quarter of the way open. Add oil to a Dutch oven, about 2 inches (5 cm) deep, cover and heat on the Egg until the oil reaches 375°F (190°C). While the oil is heating, dredge the poblanos in flour, then the egg, then into the cornmeal and set on a drying rack.

When the oil is hot, gently add 3 poblanos to the oil and fry, flipping once, for 3 to 4 minutes or until golden brown and crisp. Remove to a drying rack and repeat until finished.

ASIAN SLAW

This slaw is made with Southeast Asian flavors and is a bright and crispy complement to grilled burgers, steak, pork and fish. The slaw goes well not only with Asian dishes, but also with many grilled meats and fish. It is also good for outdoor gatherings because it does not require refrigeration.

MAKES ABOUT 8 TO 10 SERVINGS

6 cups (900 g) shredded cabbage, red, green or a mix

½ European cucumber, cut into matchsticks, 2 inches (5 cm) long

2 carrots, cut into matchsticks, 2 inches (5 cm) long

2 green onions, sliced lengthwise into strips, 1 inch (2.5 cm) long

2 tbsp (5 g) fresh cilantro, chopped

2 tbsp (30 ml) rice wine vinegar

2 tbsp (30 ml) soy sauce

2 tbsp (30 ml) toasted sesame oil

2 tbsp (30 ml) lime juice

2 tsp (6 g) granulated sugar

1 tsp freshly ground black pepper

1 tsp toasted sesame seeds

In a bowl, combine all the vegetables and herbs. In a small saucepan, heat all of the remaining ingredients except the sesame seeds. Simmer for 2 minutes to blend the flavors. Pour the mixture over the cabbage mix and stir. Cover and refrigerate, letting the slaw marinate for at least 2 hours, stirring occasionally. This can marinate overnight, but make sure you stir the ingredients well the next morning. When ready to serve, pour off any excess liquid and sprinkle with toasted sesame seeds.

CUCUMBER SALAD

This is a fast and easy side dish recipe that adds a sweet, tangy crunch to a variety of barbecue dishes. It is a great dish to prepare for a potluck or an outdoor gathering because it doesn't need to stay refrigerated.

MAKES ABOUT 10 TO 12 SERVINGS

PICKLING LIQUID

½ cup (12 ml) white vinegar

¼ cup (50 g) granulated sugar

2 tsp (5 g) celery seeds

½ tsp kosher salt

½ tsp freshly ground black pepper

½ tsp fresh garlic, minced

6 cups (900 g) cucumbers, pickling are preferred, cut into ¼-inch (6-mm) slices

1 cup (150 g) plum tomatoes, seeds removed, chopped

½ cup (75 g) Vidalia onion, diced

In a large bowl, combine all of the pickling ingredients and whisk until the sugar has dissolved. Place cucumber slices in a bowl and add tomatoes to the bowl. Add diced onions to the bowl.

Mix well, cover and refrigerate for 30 minutes to 1 hour and serve.

SWEET STUFFED VIDALIA ONIONS

Vidalia onions are sweet, and baking them on the Egg allows their sugars to start to caramelize and a hint of smoke to be added. If you prefer, you can use large yellow onions for a more pronounced onion flavor. To spice things up, try using hot Italian ground sausage or add a diced jalapeño to the mix. However you decide to make it, bacon and sausage have always been great ways to get me to eat my vegetables!

MAKES ABOUT 4 SERVINGS

4 large Vidalia onions

¼ lb (112 g) diced bacon or ground sausage

½ cup (38 g) fresh mushrooms, diced

2 tsp (6 g) garlic, minced

¼ cup (15 g) dried bread crumbs

½ cup (45 g) sharp cheddar cheese, shredded

½ tsp celery seed

½ tsp kosher salt

½ tsp black pepper

Peel the onions and cut off the tip of the roots so they stand up. Using a grapefruit spoon or a melon baller, hollow out the inside of the onions, leaving the walls of the onions about ⅓ inch (8 mm) thick. Chop half the removed onion pieces into small dice and set aside.

In a medium frying pan, brown the bacon or sausage until cooked. Drain the bacon or sausage, reserving the fat. Return 2 tablespoons (30 ml) of the fat to the frying pan with the chopped onion and the mushrooms. Sauté until the onions and mushrooms start to soften, about 5 minutes. Add the minced garlic and continue to sauté until the garlic is softened, but not browned, about 2 minutes more. Add the bread crumbs, shredded cheese, drained bacon or sausage, celery seed, salt and pepper. Stir on the heat until the cheese starts to melt, and then remove from the heat.

Rub the outside of the onions with the reserved bacon fat and sprinkle with salt and pepper. Stuff the onions with the mixture. Place the stuffed onions on a baking sheet or in a casserole dish.

Set the Egg for 350°F (180°C) indirect. With the top and bottom vents wide open, light the fire and close the Egg. When the Egg gets up to about 250°F (121°C) dome, about 10 minutes, close the bottom screen. When the Egg approaches 350°F (180°C) dome, about 10 minutes, slide the top of the daisy wheel partially closed, leaving it a quarter of the way open.

When the Egg is up to temperature, place the onions on the Egg and cook until the onions soften, about 30 minutes. Remove and serve.

GRILLED FENNEL AND ORANGE SALAD

Grilling most vegetables will enhance their flavors and add a smoky accent. The orange pairs well with the fennel's licorice notes. This salad will go well with any meat, fish or poultry. For a variation, grill some halved cherry tomatoes and add them to the salad.

MAKES ABOUT 4 TO 6 SERVINGS

4 bulbs fennel

¼ cup (60 ml) olive oil

¼ cup (60 ml) white wine vinegar

1 tbsp (15 ml) lime juice

1 tsp minced garlic

¼ tsp kosher salt

Pinch fresh ground black pepper

6 clementines or 3 large navel oranges

Set the Egg for 350°F (180°C) direct. With the top and bottom vents wide open, light the fire and close the Egg. When the Egg gets up to about 250°F (121°C) dome, about 10 minutes, close the bottom screen. When the Egg approaches 350°F (180°C) dome, about 10 minutes, slide the top of the daisy wheel partially closed, leaving it a quarter of the way open. Prepare the fennel by cutting off the root end and removing any discolored or torn leaves. Cut off and reserve the fronds. Cut bulbs lengthwise into ½-inch (12-mm) slices. In a small bowl, mix the olive oil, vinegar, lime juice, garlic, salt and pepper together. Brush each side of the sliced fennel bulbs with the liquid mixture.

Peel the clementines and remove any pith or seeds. Slice in half and put into a bowl to hold the juices. If using navel oranges, slice off the peels and the outer skin on the individual sections. Remove any pith or seeds. Slice each section into thirds and place to a bowl to hold the juices.

When the Egg is up to temperature, place the fennel slices across the grate and cook for about 10 minutes, turning once, until the slices are tender and a little charred. Remove from the Egg and drizzle with leftover vinegar mixture, add the orange slices with the juice and the reserved fronds, toss and serve.

SWEET POTATO SANDWICHES

Sweet potatoes don't necessarily sound like a great snack component. This recipe, however, has impressed everyone who has tried it. We won first place in Lake Placid with this recipe, along with Coffee Encrusted Pork Tenderloin. The winnings paid for the flight for our Hawaii trip, as if it wasn't special enough!

MAKES ABOUT 4 SERVINGS

2 sweet potatoes, about 2 inch (5 cm) in uniform diameter

2 tbsp (30 ml) olive oil

1 cup (240 g) cream cheese, softened

¼ cup (60 ml) pepper jelly

¼ cup (40 g) dried cranberries, chopped

2 tbsp (30 g) Pork Rub (page 206)

¼ cup (40 g) pecans

Peel and cut the sweet potatoes into ¼-inch (6-mm) slices. Set the Egg for 350°F (180°C), direct, and use either the half-round cast-iron griddle grate, or a cast-iron frying-pan that will fit on your Egg. With the top and bottom vents wide open, light the fire and close the Egg. When the Egg gets up to about 250°F (121°C) dome, about 10 minutes, close the bottom screen. When the Egg approaches 350°F (180°C) dome, about 10 minutes, slide the top of the daisy wheel partially closed, leaving it a quarter of the way open. Add olive oil to coat the bottom of a griddle or pan and when hot, add the sliced sweet potatoes. Cook for 3 to 4 minutes per side, using the double spatula method turning once, until golden brown. Remove from heat to a rack to drain.

Mix the cream cheese, pepper jelly and cranberries together, spread about 1 tablespoon (15 g) on a slice of potato, sprinkle with rub and add some pecans on top. Add a dollop of cream cheese mixture to another potato slice to help it to adhere to the bottom and place the slice on top to make a sandwich. Serve at room temperature.

CHIMICHURRI STEAK SAUCE

Chimichurri is a sauce originating from Argentina and served with grilled meats, especially beef.
It is used in Argentina like we use ketchup in the United States. It can be used as a marinade,
and other variations include fresh cilantro, diced jalapeños or a pinch of cayenne.
Its flavors accent the grilled meat well and a little goes a long way.

MAKES ABOUT 1 CUP (240 ML), OR 4 TO 6 SERVINGS

½ cup (120 ml) olive oil

3 tbsp (45 ml) red wine vinegar

1 tbsp (15 ml) lime juice

2 tsp (6 g) fresh garlic, minced

1 tsp kosher salt

1 tsp freshly ground black pepper

1 tsp crushed red pepper flakes

1 cup (40 g) flat leaf parsley, chopped

½ cup (20 g) fresh oregano leaves, chopped

In a large bowl, mix all of the ingredients together except the fresh herbs. Whisk well, until ingredients are incorporated. Add the fresh herbs and mix thoroughly. For best results, refrigerate for 1 hour before serving.

TOMATO JAM

I really like bottled tomato ketchup with burgers, hot dogs, fries and beans, but it is a little sweet. This tomato jam is not as sweet and has a lot more depth of flavor and spiciness. It can be used in place of ketchup, but it also tastes great on toast or bagels.

MAKES ABOUT 1 CUP (237 ML)

3 tbsp (45 ml) olive oil

⅓ cup (66 g) onion, minced

1 tsp garlic, minced

2 lb (900 g) Roma tomatoes, seeds and core removed, chopped

½ cup (90 g) brown sugar

3 tbsp (45 ml) lime juice

2 tbsp (30 ml) apple cider vinegar

1 tsp kosher salt

1 tsp freshly ground black pepper

1 tsp dry mustard

1 tsp chipotle powder

½ tsp ground cumin

Set up the Egg for 300°F (150°C) indirect. With the top and bottom vents wide open, light the fire and close the Egg. When the Egg gets up to about 250°F (121°C) dome, about 10 minutes, close the bottom screen. Place the olive oil in a nonreactive saucepan on the grate. When the Egg approaches 300°F (150°C) dome, about 5 minutes, slide the top of the daisy wheel partially closed, leaving it a quarter of the way open. When the Egg is up to temperature, add the minced onion to the pan and sauté the onion for about 5 minutes, until softened but not toasted. Add the garlic and sauté for 1 minute longer. Add the remaining ingredients and leaving the pan uncovered, close the Egg. Let the jam simmer for 1 to 1½ hours, stirring every 15 minutes. If the jam isn't simmering after the first 15 minutes, increase the temperature of the Egg to 400°F (200°C) until simmering. Reduce the temperature back down to 300°F (150°C) to continue simmering. After about 1 hour, mash the jam with a potato masher to break up the pieces into a chunky/pasty consistency. When the jam has thickened, remove it from the Egg and pour it into a dish to cool. Refrigerate or serve.

ROASTED GARLIC

Not everyone loves garlic, but those who do can't get enough of it. However, to some,
fresh garlic can be too strong for their liking, and overcooked garlic can taste burned and acrid.
Roasting the garlic tames it so that it is sweet, nutty, soft and smooth. You can spread it on toast,
or just squeeze it into your mouth, as long as you don't cook it too long.

MAKES ABOUT 8 SERVINGS

4 heads garlic

2 tbsp (30 ml) olive oil

Remove the outer paper layer from the garlic heads, but do not separate the individual cloves. With a sharp knife or a pair of kitchen shears, snip off the top end of each clove.

Set the Egg for 350°F (180°C) indirect with a drip pan. With the top and bottom vents wide open, light the fire and close the Egg. When the Egg gets up to about 250°F (121°C) dome, about 10 minutes, close the bottom screen. When the Egg approaches 350°F (180°C) dome, about 10 minutes, slide the top of the daisy wheel partially closed, leaving it a quarter of the way open. When the Egg is up to temperature, place the trimmed heads root-side down on the grate, and drizzle with olive oil. Roast the garlic until it is soft, about 45 minutes. When cooked, separate the individual cloves to squeeze out the garlic paste.

★ CHAPTER 7 ★

BETTER THAN A BRICK OVEN— BREADS & PIZZAS ON THE EGG

The Egg is an excellent "brick" oven. It retains moisture while baking and is capable of high temperatures for developing a moist crust. The brick-oven effect also imparts wood-fired brick-oven flavors to bread and pizza. It is a subtle smoky flavor, but you can really appreciate the difference over just oven-baked. Cooking bread outdoors won't heat up your house and can be done year-round. When it comes to bread and pizza on the Egg, it's all positive!

CHEDDAR CHEESE STRAWS

Usually cheese straws are made by piping them through a cookie press and then cutting them into shorter lengths. This recipe skips that step, so you not only cut down the preparation time, but you also get to enjoy these elegant, crunchy appetizers much sooner! You can use a food processor a stand mixer or work the dough by hand. They are a great snack for children of all ages.

MAKES ABOUT 48 PIECES

1⅔ cups (207 g) all-purpose flour

1 tsp kosher salt

1 tsp dry mustard

½ tsp cayenne pepper

½ cup (120 ml) unsalted butter, cut into small pieces

1 tsp Worcestershire sauce

8 oz (225 g) extra sharp cheddar cheese, grated

2 tbsp (30 ml) water

Mix together the flour, salt, dry mustard and cayenne pepper in a bowl. Put the cubed butter, the Worcestershire sauce and the cheddar cheese in a mixing bowl and combine for several minutes, until thoroughly blended. Gradually add the dry ingredients to the cheese mixture and mix well. Add the water and mix for 1 minute longer.

Turn the dough out onto a well-floured surface and knead it a few times. Using a well-floured rolling pin, roll the dough out to ¼-inch (6-mm) thick. Using a pizza cutter or a sharp knife, cut the dough into strips, ¼ inch (6 mm) wide and 5 inches (13 cm) in length.

Place the strips on ungreased baking sheets, ½ inch (12 mm) apart.

Set the Egg up for 425°F (220°C) indirect with a raised rack. With the top and bottom vents wide open, light the fire and close the Egg. When the Egg gets up to about 250°F (121°C) dome, about 10 minutes, close the bottom screen. When the Egg approaches 425°F (220°C) dome, about 10 to 12 minutes, slide the top of the daisy wheel partially closed, leaving it halfway open. Place the baking sheet on the rack and bake for 12 to 16 minutes, until golden brown and crisp. Eat when cooled completely and store in an air-tight container.

WHOLE WHEAT PITA BREAD

There are so many ways to enjoy pita bread—stuffed with roasted vegetables, meats and cheeses, and even as a "holder" for fruits. These are so much better tasting than the store bought pita rounds. After baking, you can slice them into wedges, brush with infused olive oil and sprinkle the slices with garlic salt or your favorite rub. Return them to the Egg for an additional 5 or 6 minutes. The choices are endless!

MAKES ABOUT 6 SERVINGS

1 package (7 g) active dry yeast

1 tbsp (12 g) granulated sugar

1 cup (240 ml) warm water 105°F to 115°F (41°C to 46°C)

1½ cups (187 g) all-purpose flour

½ tsp kosher salt

1½ cups (195 g) whole wheat flour

In a large bowl of a stand mixer fitted with a dough hook, combine the yeast, sugar and warm water. Stir to blend, and then let the yeast stand until foamy, about 5 to 10 minutes. Add in the all-purpose flour and the salt and beat at a low speed until smooth. Gradually add in the whole wheat flour, a little at a time at lowest speed, until the flour is incorporated and the dough gathers into a ball. This should take about 4 minutes.

Turn the dough out onto a well-floured surface and knead until it is smooth and elastic, about 3 minutes. Cover the dough with a towel and let it rest for 10 minutes. Transfer the dough to a lightly oiled bowl, turning it to coat, and cover with plastic wrap. Allow the dough to rise until doubled in size, about 1½ hours.

Set the Egg for 375°F (190°C) direct with a pizza stone on the grate. With the top and bottom vents wide open, light the fire and close the Egg. When the Egg gets up to about 250°F (121°C) dome, about 10 minutes, close the bottom screen and add a pizza stone on an elevated rack. When the Egg approaches 375°F (190°C) dome, about 10 minutes, slide the top of the daisy wheel partially closed, leaving it a quarter of the way open.

Punch the dough down and divide it into 6 equal portions. Shape each portion into a smooth ball, keeping all of them lightly floured and covered while you work. Allow the balls to rest for about 10 minutes, to make them easier to roll out, and then pat or roll each ball into a 5-inch (12-cm) very thin circle.

Place the circles on the preheated pizza stone, 2 or 3 at a time, and bake for 8 to 10 minutes. Watch the bread carefully, making sure it is not burning. It will puff up like a balloon and will be pale golden in color. Remove the bread from the Egg and place on a cooling rack for 5 minutes. They will deflate during this time, leaving a nice pocket in the center.

CIABATTA BREAD

This bread is really easy to make and is perfectly crusty on the outside and chewy on the inside. It can be sliced to dip in infused olive oil, spread with butter or sliced lengthwise for a crunchy sandwich. The hardest part of this bread recipe is waiting long enough for the bread to cool before eating it!

MAKES 1 LOAF

3¼ cups (323 g) all-purpose flour

1½ tsp (4.7 g) active dry yeast

1 tsp kosher salt

¾ tsp granulated sugar

1¾ cups plus 2 tbsp (420 ml plus 30 ml) warm 115°F (46°C) water

2 tsp (10 ml) olive oil

In the bowl of a stand mixer, whisk together the flour, yeast, salt and sugar. Pour in the warm water and beat for 5 minutes, until the dough is well combined. When combined, turn off the mixer, flour your hands and reach into the bowl, pulling and pushing the dough up and down to push air bubbles into the dough to create nice holes when it bakes.

Oil a large bowl and place the dough into the bowl. Drizzle the olive oil over the top of the dough, and then cover the bowl with plastic wrap, and then a dish towel. Place the bowl in a warm spot to rise for about 2 hours.

Set your Egg for 400°F (200°C) indirect. With the top and bottom vents wide open, light the fire and close the Egg. When the Egg gets up to about 250°F (121°C) dome, about 10 minutes, add a pizza stone on a raised rack and close the bottom screen. When the Egg approaches 400°F (200°C) dome, about 10 to 12 minutes, slide the top of the daisy wheel partially closed, leaving it a quarter of the way open. If no pizza stone is available, line a baking sheet that will fit on the Egg with parchment paper, then sprinkle it with flour.

When the Egg is up to temperature, flour your hands, and shape the dough into a long loaf, about 12 inches by 4 inches (30 by 10 cm) wide. Sprinkle the top of the loaf with flour and place the loaf on the preheated pizza stone, or place the loaf on the prepared baking sheet and place it on the Egg. Bake for 35 to 40 minutes, until lightly golden. When the bread is tapped, it should sound hollow. That is how you know it's ready.

Remove the bread to a rack and allow it to cool for at least 30 minutes before slicing.

CORN TORTILLAS

Tortillas are made of either corn or flour. Flour tortillas are found more in the Northern parts of Mexico and corn in the Central and Southern regions. Corn, however, gives the most authentic flavor and texture and can be used for tacos, tostadas, enchiladas, quesadillas and tortilla chips. This recipe has basic ingredients and uses a tortilla press to form the corn tortillas. They are cooked on a griddle or cast iron pan to give them a slightly crispy texture and slightly toasted corn flavor.

MAKES ABOUT 12, 5- TO 6-INCH (13- TO 15-CM) IN DIAMETER TORTILLAS

2 cups (114 g) masa harina
1¼ cups (300 ml) warm water
¼ tsp table salt

Mix all of the ingredients together in a medium bowl and mix for about 3 minutes to form a dough. Add more water if the mix seems too brittle, more masa harina if the mix seems too wet. Cover and let it sit at room temperature for 1 hour. After an hour, divide the mix into 12 round balls. Place a piece of a large resealable plastic bag on the bottom of the press. Place the dough ball in the center of the press on top of the plastic and press down a little with the palm of your hand. Lay a second piece of plastic bag on top of the dough and close the press, a few times if necessary, to get a thin round.

Set up the Egg for 350°F (180°C) direct with a griddle pan or cast-iron pan that fits into the Egg. With the top and bottom vents wide open, light the fire and close the Egg. When the Egg gets up to about 250°F (121°C) dome, about 10 minutes, close the bottom screen. When the Egg approaches 350°F (180°C) dome, about 10 minutes, slide the top of the daisy wheel closed, keeping the daisy wheel petals a quarter of the way open.

Lift the tortillas out of the press and peel off the top plastic layer. Flip in your hand and remove the bottom piece of plastic and place the tortillas in the griddle pan. Cook for about 1 minute per side, until the tortilla is browned but not burned, using a spatula or butter knife to flip. Remove the tortillas from the pan to a rack to cool for 2 minutes, then stack together and cover the pile in a towel to stay warm.

NAAN

Naan is a flat bread found in the cuisines of west central and south Asia. It is quick to make and goes great with soups and stews, wraps and kabobs. You can even use it for flatbread pizzas.

MAKES ABOUT 8 SERVINGS

1 cup (240 ml) very warm water, 120°F to 130°F (49°C to 54°C)

2 tsp (8 g) granulated sugar

2¼ tsp (7 g) instant yeast

3 to 4 cups (297 to 396 g) all-purpose flour

⅓ cup (80 ml) plain yogurt

3 tbsp (45 ml) milk

3 tbsp (45 ml) butter, melted

1 tsp table salt

Vegetable oil for shaping

Stir water and sugar in a large bowl. Add the yeast and let it sit until it is foamy, about 10 minutes.

Add flour, yogurt, milk, melted butter and salt and stir until a soft dough forms. The dough will be sticky to touch. Drizzle 1 teaspoon vegetable oil on top of the dough and cover the bowl with a damp cloth. Place the bowl in a warm place and allow the dough to rise until doubled in size, about 1 hour.

On a floured work surface, knead the dough 8 to 10 times, divide the dough into 8 equal pieces, and roll into balls using oiled hands. Cover and allow to rise for 15 to 20 minutes.

Coating your hands with vegetable oil, shape each dough ball by flattening it and then gently stretching and pulling edges to about ⅛ inch to ¼ inch (3 to 6 mm) thick.

Set the Egg for 375°F (190°C) direct. With the top and bottom vents wide open, light the fire and close the Egg. When the Egg gets up to about 250°F (121°C) dome, about 10 minutes, close the bottom screen. When the Egg approaches 375°F (180°C) dome, about 10 minutes, slide the top of the daisy wheel partially closed, leaving it a quarter of the way open. Preheat a griddle or heavy bottomed skillet on the grate. Lightly oil griddle or pan. Place flattened dough pieces onto heated cooking surface and cook for 1 to 2 minutes per side. The flatbreads are ready to turn when large bubbles appear on the top surface. The bottom surface should be lightly browned.

Transfer to a plate and serve immediately or cool to room temperature and store in an airtight container for up to 1 week.

CHERRY TOMATO AND FETA CHEESE PIZZA WITH SMOKIN' ACES' FAMOUS PIZZA DOUGH

Pizza on the Egg is a common activity for Eggheads. Whether it's a single pizza for dinner
or a weekly pizza party, they are the best! The dough for this recipe appeared in my first book, *Smoke It
Like a Pro*, contributed by Chuck and Nancy Helwig of the Championship Smokin' Aces Barbecue Team
from Chicopee, Massachusetts. Chuck and Nancy have made countless pizzas on their Big Green Eggs,
whether in grilling competitions, cooking demos or on their deck at home. Nothing beats
the taste of a wood-fired pizza, and nothing beats their pizza dough.

MAKES 6 TO 8 SERVINGS

PIZZA DOUGH

4¼ cups (531 g) flour

2¼ tsp (7 g) yeast, or one packet of yeast

1½ tsp (9 g) table salt

2 tsp (8 g) sugar

2 tbsp (30 ml) olive oil

1¾ cups (420 ml) warm water

TOPPING FOR 2 PIZZAS

2 pt (960 g) cherry or grape tomatoes, sliced in half sideways

1 cup (90 g) feta cheese, crumbled

1 cup (40 g) fresh basil leaves

¼ cup (60 ml) garlic-infused olive oil

½ tsp kosher salt

½ tsp freshly ground black pepper

Put all dry ingredients in a food processor with the dough hook on. Pulse the dry
ingredients 3 to 4 times.

Turn on food processor and slowly add the olive oil, then slowly add the warm water
until a ball forms and the dough is sticky to the touch. Turn off the food processor
and let the dough rest for 2 minutes. Turn on the food processor again for 30 to
40 seconds, then place the dough in a well-oiled bowl and let it rise. If planning
to use the dough the next day, place it in an oiled resealable bag and put it in the
refrigerator, where it will rise overnight. This recipe makes 2 pizza crusts. You can
multiply the recipe and freeze additional dough balls for future use.

For the Egg setup you will not need your grill grate. Put the plate setter in the Egg
with the legs down and place a pizza stone on top. To prevent the pizza from sticking,
let the plate setter and stone warm up to temperature before putting the pizza on to
cook. Cook the pizza between 550°F (288°C) dome and 600°F (316°C) dome. With
the top and bottom vents wide open, light the fire and close the Egg. When the Egg
gets up to about 250°F (121°C) dome, about 10 minutes, close the bottom screen.
When the Egg approaches 550°F (288°C) dome, about 12 to 15 minutes, slide the
top of the daisy wheel partially closed, keeping it half open.

Flour a cutting board and roll out your crust. Spread cornmeal on a pizza peel and
carefully lift the crust onto that. Spread one half of the tomatoes, cut side up and
sprinkle with half of the feta and half of the basil. Drizzle with half of the garlic oil
and sprinkle with half of the salt and half of the pepper. Open your Egg and carefully
slide the pizza off of the peel onto the pizza stone using a slight shaking motion.

Close the cover and check after about 6 minutes. You may need to reposition the pizza
for even cooking. When it is done, slide it back onto the peel and transfer to a cutting
board. Repeat for the second pizza. Allow it to cool for a few minutes before slicing.

RUSTIC COUNTRY BREAD

This recipe makes 1 large, oval loaf of chewy goodness. Baking it on a pizza stone assures a crispy crust. You can vary the flavors by adding fresh herbs, such as rosemary or thyme, or dried fruits or nuts. The possibilities are endless!

MAKES 2, 10-INCH (25-CM) LOAVES OR 1 DOUBLE LOAF

SPONGE STARTER

1 cup (130 g) whole wheat flour

½ cup (50 g) bread flour

½ tsp instant yeast

1¼ cups (300 ml) lukewarm water (90°F to 100°F [32°C to 38°C])

DOUGH

½ tsp rapid rise yeast

1 cup (240 ml) lukewarm water (90°F to 100°F [32°C to 38°C])

2 tbsp (30 ml) honey

1½ tsp (7 g) table salt

2¼ cups (281 g) bread flour

½ cup (45 g) rye flour

⅓ cup (56 g) cornmeal

2 tbsp (16 g) toasted wheat germ

⅓ cup (27 g) rolled oats

Rolled oats for top

For the sponge starter, stir together the whole wheat flour, the bread flour and the yeast in a medium bowl. Stir in the water until the consistency is like a thick cake batter. Cover the bowl loosely with plastic wrap and let it sit overnight, or up to 24 hours, at room temperature.

To make the dough, dissolve the yeast in lukewarm water in a large bowl. Using a wooden spoon, mix in the sponge starter, honey and salt until thoroughly blended. Add 2 cups (250 g) of the bread flour (reserving ¼ cup [31 g]), the rye flour, cornmeal, wheat germ and rolled oats and stir until combined. If the dough is too sticky, mix in the remaining bread flour. Cover with plastic wrap and rest for 20 minutes. You will need to "turn" the dough several turns by sliding your hand down the edge of the bowl and lifting and stretching the dough up and over the center. Cover and let the dough rest for another 30 minutes. Repeat turning and resting a few more times for a total of 2 hours rising time.

Shape the loaf by turning it out on a lightly floured surface. With floured hands, divide the dough by half and press to deflate the dough. Shape each half into an oval by pulling an edge of the dough from the outside to the center and proceed by turning clockwise, repeating the process 6 or 7 times. The inside edges will form a seam. Cover and rest the loaves for 20 minutes.

Working with the seam-side up, slightly flatten the dough Repeat the above shaping process one more time, going all the way around the loaf and shaping the dough into a ball. Cover and let the dough rise, seam-side up, on a piece of parchment paper generously dusted with bread flour, for 1½ to 2 hours.

Set the Egg for 475°F (240°C) indirect. With the top and bottom vents wide open, light the fire and close the Egg. When the Egg gets up to about 250°F (121°C) dome, about 10 minutes, place a pizza stone on a raised rack and close the bottom screen. When the Egg approaches 475°F (240°C) dome, about 10 to 15 minutes, slide the top of the daisy wheel partially closed, leaving it halfway open. When the Egg is up to temperature and baking 1 loaf at a time, place the loaf seam-side down on a piece of parchment paper. Brush the top lightly with water and sprinkle the oats on top. Using a sharp knife, score the top of the loaves. Carefully slide the loaf with the parchment paper onto the preheated baking stone. Bake for 20 to 30 minutes, to an internal temperature of 200°F (93°C). Remove to a wire rack to cool before slicing. If you desire, you can combine the dough before baking and make one very impressive loaf.

CHAPTER 8

COMFORTING SLOW COOKED CASSEROLES, BRAISES & STEWS

One might not think there is any advantage to cooking casseroles or stews on the Egg, but there is. First, you can set the temperature to a simmer, and if you leave the cover off of the pot, you will get some smoke flavor as the soup or stew simmers. Second, you don't need to heat up your house, and you don't need to tend to the stove if you want to be outside socializing or puttering around. Last, they are all great side dishes to everything you cook on the Egg.

CHEESY SCALLOPED POTATOES

This dish is a perfect side dish to any roasted or grilled meat. I grew up eating scalloped potatoes on holidays and sweet potatoes on Thanksgiving. We always had cheese in the refrigerator. I like sweet potatoes even more than I like white potatoes. This recipe puts them all together in the perfect blend.

MAKES ABOUT 6 TO 8 SERVINGS

3 large white potatoes

3 large sweet potatoes

1 cup (240 ml) milk

1 cup (240 ml) heavy cream

2 tbsp (23 g) dark brown sugar

1 tsp garlic powder

½ tsp kosher salt

Pinch ground black pepper

Pinch nutmeg

Pinch white pepper

¼ cup (60 ml) unsalted butter, softened

2 cups (180 g) sharp cheddar cheese, grated

Set the Egg for 350°F (180°C) indirect with a raised grate. With the top and bottom vents wide open, light the fire and close the Egg. When the Egg gets up to about 250°F (121°C) dome, about 10 minutes, close the bottom screen. When the Egg approaches 350°F (180°C) dome, about 10 minutes, slide the top of the daisy wheel partially closed, leaving it a quarter of the way open. Wash, peel and slice the potatoes into ¼-inch (6-mm) slices. In a large bowl, add all ingredients except the cheese and stir until blended. Grease the bottom and sides of a 9- by 12-inch (23- by 30-cm) casserole dish with butter. Lay one layer of potatoes across the bottom, and then add about a quarter of the mixture. Sprinkle with a quarter of the grated cheese. Repeat these layers until all the ingredients are in the casserole, finishing with a layer of cheese.

When the Egg is up to temperature, place the casserole on a raised rack and cook for about 50 minutes, until the potatoes are tender. When cooked, remove from the Egg and serve.

UN-DEBATABLE BRUNSWICK STEW

There exists a forever debate as to where Brunswick Stew originated from—Brunswick County, Virginia, or Brunswick, Georgia. There is, however, no debate that it is a great accompaniment to delicious barbecue, or as a meal itself, no matter where it originated from!

SERVES 12 AS A SIDE DISH OR 6 AS A MEAL

2 tbsp (30 ml) olive oil

1 cup (150 g) onion, chopped

1 tbsp (9 g) garlic, minced

3 lb (1.4 kg) chicken legs, wings, breasts, bone-in, skin-on

2 lb (900 g) pork shoulder or country-style ribs from the butt end

2 qt (1.9 L) warm water

1 tsp kosher salt

1 tsp freshly ground black pepper

¼ tsp cayenne pepper

2 cups (300 g) tomatoes, chopped

1½ cups (225 g) sliced celery with leaves

1½ cups (225 g) potatoes, peeled and diced

1 tbsp (15 ml) Worcestershire sauce

1 cup (150 g) corn kernels, fresh or canned

1 cup (150 g) lima beans, frozen or canned

Set up the Egg for 400°F (200°C) indirect. With the top and bottom vents wide open, light the fire and close the Egg. When the Egg gets up to about 250°F (121°C) dome, about 10 minutes, close the bottom screen and set the Dutch oven on the grate. When the Egg approaches 400°F (200°C) dome, about 10 minutes, slide the top of the daisy wheel closed, leaving the petals a quarter of the way open. When the Egg is up to temperature, add olive oil and the onion and sauté for about 5 minutes until softened but not toasted. Add the garlic and sauté for about 1 minute. Remove the onion and garlic and add the chicken and pork to brown on all sides, about 10 minutes. You may need to brown the chicken and pork separately because of the size of the Dutch oven.

When the meat has browned, add the water, onion, garlic, salt, black pepper and cayenne pepper. Cover and bring to a boil. When the pot is boiling, close the daisy wheel petals to about half open for all the meat to simmer. Simmer for an hour, then remove the pork and chicken with a slotted spoon and set aside, Add the tomatoes, celery, potatoes and Worcestershire sauce, and simmer uncovered for an hour, stirring occasionally. Shred the chicken, discarding the skin and bones. Chunk the pork and discard any large pieces of fat or any bones. Add the meat to the Dutch oven and continue to simmer for an additional 30 minutes, stirring occasionally.

Add the corn and lima beans and simmer for 20 minutes, adding water if necessary. The stew should be fairly thick. Taste and add additional salt, pepper or Worcestershire sauce, spoon into bowls and serve.

See photo on page 174.

BLACK BEANS

This recipe for black beans has additional spices and ingredients to make a great side dish. Alternately, the beans can be added to rice, tacos or salads for additional flavor and texture.

MAKES 4 TO 6 SERVINGS

4 oz (112 g) piece salt pork, diced into ¼-inch (6-mm) cubes

½ cup (76 g) onion, chopped

1 tbsp (9 g) garlic, minced

½ tsp cumin

½ tsp dried oregano

1 tsp chili powder

1 tsp kosher salt

1 tbsp (15 ml) Worcestershire sauce

½ tsp black pepper

3 cups (603 g) dry black beans

3 qt (2.9 L) hot water

Set up the Egg for 300°F (150°C) indirect. With the top and bottom vents wide open, light the fire and close the Egg. When the Egg gets up to about 250°F (121°C) dome, about 10 minutes, set the Dutch oven on the grate and close the bottom screen. When the Egg approaches 300°F (150°C) dome, about 7 minutes, slide the top of the daisy wheel closed, leaving the petals open. When the Egg is up to temperature, add the cubed salt pork to the Dutch oven and fry it until slightly crisp. Set aside the salt pork and all but 2 tablespoons (30 ml) of the rendered fat. Cook the onion and garlic for about 5 minutes until softened but not toasted. Add the remaining ingredients, except the beans and water and mix for 2 minutes. Remove from the Dutch oven and add it to the drained salt pork. Add the beans and water to the Dutch oven and cover, closing the Egg. Let the beans simmer for 2 to 2½ hours. If the beans are not simmering after the first 15 minutes, increase the temperature of the Egg to 400°F (200°C) until simmering. Reduce the temperature back down to 300°F (150°C) to continue simmering. When the beans are cooked through, but still fairly firm, skim off any remaining water, add the reserved ingredients and stir for 5 minutes. Remove from the Egg and serve, or refrigerate for later use. As an alternative, the beans can be soaked overnight and cooked in the soaking water. This will reduce the simmering time by about an hour.

★ **CHAPTER 9** ★

JUST DESSERTS

Desserts on the Egg are not necessarily just sweet endings. Some are meant as snacks, and others require the pitmaster to perform quality control. This always reduces the availability for the end of the meal. As with all recipes cooked on the Egg, and over charcoal, the hint of smoke, whether grilled or baked, is a pleasing dimension of flavor. A word of caution: Don't be the last in line.

MAPLE BACON BAKLAVA

My wife, Cindi, has made this recipe several times for grilling competitions, and we have done great with it. Traditional baklava will use honey in addition to granulated white sugar for the sauce. This recipe, however, uses maple syrup and brown sugar for the sweetness. A little bit of cayenne pepper balances the sweetness, and, oh yeah, we've included BACON!

MAKES 40 TO 48 SERVINGS

1 lb (450 g) package frozen phyllo dough

1½ cups (360 ml) unsalted butter, melted

2 cups (300 g) walnuts, finely chopped

2 cups (300 g) pecans, finely chopped

1 lb (450 g) cooked maple bacon, finely chopped

½ cup (90 g) dark brown sugar

1 cup (240 ml) pure maple syrup, grade B if available

1 tsp ground cinnamon

½ tsp cayenne pepper

¼ cup (60 ml) water

Thaw phyllo at room temperature for about 2 hours. Cut in half crosswise and cover with plastic wrap or wax paper to keep it from drying out.

Butter the bottom of a 9- by 13-inch (23- by 32-cm) baking dish. Place 1 sheet of the phyllo in the dish and brush it carefully with melted butter. Add 6 more sheets, brushing each with butter.

In a bowl, combine the nuts, bacon and brown sugar. Sprinkle about 1 cup (150 g) over the pastry. Top with 4 more sheets of phyllo, brushing each sheet with butter. Sprinkle on another cup (150 g) of the bacon mixture. Repeat, layering the 4 sheets, nut mixture and butter until 8 sheets phyllo remain. Place these on the top, brushing each with melted butter.

With a sharp knife, cut 1-inch (2.5-cm) squares, cutting to (but not through) the bottom layer. Continue cutting at 1-inch (2.5-cm) spacing until you have about 48 pieces.

Set the Egg for 350°F (180°C) indirect with a raised rack. With the top and bottom vents wide open, light the fire and close the Egg. When the Egg gets up to about 250°F (121°C) dome, about 10 minutes, close the bottom screen. When the Egg approaches 350°F (180°C) dome, about 10 minutes, slide the top of the daisy wheel partially closed, leaving it a quarter of the way open. Bake for 30 to 40 minutes, rotating the pan halfway through the cook time. Remove from the Egg, finish cutting through the squares and cool.

While the pastry cools, warm the syrup, cinnamon, cayenne pepper and water in a small saucepan for about 10 minutes. Pour the warmed syrup over the cooled pastry and allow it to set for about an hour before serving.

MILK CHOCOLATE COCONUT CHUNK COOKIES

These cookies can be made with your choice of chocolate chips, but in our house the cookies are always made with milk chocolate. Using chunks rather than chips gives you a big, gooey bite of chocolate. These have a great chewy center from the addition of the coconut, with a nice crispy edge. The cookie dough can also be frozen for up to 3 months. As an alternative to cookies, you can also use half of the dough to make bars, by spreading the dough on a lightly greased jelly roll pan and cooking for 20 minutes. This recipe is cooked on a Himalayan Salt Rock for an additional subtle saltiness to each bite. As an alternative, it can be cooked indirect on a cookie sheet on a raised rack.

MAKES ABOUT 75 COOKIES

5 cups (989 g) chocolate chunks or chips

2 cups (152 g) sweetened coconut, shredded

2 cups (300g) almonds, chopped

4½ cups (562 g) all-purpose flour

2 tsp (8.5 g) baking soda

1 tsp salt

2 sticks unsalted butter, room temperature

1½ cups (300 g) granulated sugar

1½ cups (270 g) brown sugar

4 large eggs

1 tbsp (15 ml) vanilla

Mix the chocolate chips, coconut and almonds in a bowl and set aside. Combine all of the dry ingredients in another bowl. In a stand mixer, cream the butter and sugars together. Beat in the eggs, one at a time, and then stir in the vanilla. Stir in the dry ingredients until well mixed, and then stir in the chocolate chips, coconut and almonds. Drop, using a rounded tablespoon, onto a lightly greased cookie sheet.

Set the Egg for 400°F (200°C) direct. With the top and bottom vents wide open, light the fire and close the Egg. When the Egg gets up to about 250°F (121°C) dome, set the 2-inch (5-cm) salt block on a raised rack so it is more up in the dome of the Egg. Let the salt block come up to temperature along with the Egg, about 10 minutes, and close the bottom screen. When the Egg approaches 400°F (200°C) dome, about 10 to 15 minutes, slide the top of the daisy wheel partially closed, leaving it half of the way open.

Alternately, set the Egg for 375°F (190°C) indirect with a raised rack. With the top and bottom vents wide open, light the fire and close the Egg. When the Egg gets up to about 250°F (121°C) dome, about 10 minutes, close the bottom screen. When the Egg approaches 375°F (190°C) dome, about 10 to 12 minutes, slide the top of the daisy wheel partially closed, leaving it a quarter of the way open. When the Egg is up to temperature, place cookies on the top rack and bake for 8 to 10 minutes. Cool the cookies on the baking sheet for 5 minutes before removing to a wire rack to cool completely.

PERFECT PECANS

Toasted pecans go well as a snack or with your favorite cocktail. They don't take long to make and you can slip them in to cook during or after an afternoon of cooking with your Egg. For a substitute, you can also toast walnuts, almonds or even peanuts.

MAKES ABOUT 4 SERVINGS

¼ cup (60 ml) unsalted butter

⅓ cup (65 g) turbinado sugar

½ tsp cayenne pepper

2 tsp (4 g) cinnamon

¼ tsp black pepper

4 cups (450 g) raw pecans

½ tsp kosher salt

Set the Egg for 350°F (180°C) indirect with a drip pan. With the top and bottom vents wide open, light the fire and close the Egg. When the Egg gets up to about 250°F (121°C) dome, about 10 minutes, close the bottom screen. When the Egg approaches 350°F (180°C) dome, about 10 minutes, slide the top of the daisy wheel partially closed, leaving it a quarter of the way open.

Melt the butter in a saucepan and add all of the spices except the salt and simmer for 2 minutes to blend, being careful not to brown the butter.

When the Egg is up to temperature, place the nuts on a cookie sheet and toast them on the Egg for 5 to 7 minutes. After the pecans have toasted, add them to the butter mixture and coat them well.

Place the coated pecans back on the cookie sheet and return them to the Egg for an additional 8 to 10 minutes, turning them once. Remove from the Egg, sprinkle them with salt and let them cool. Remove from the cookie sheet when cooled and serve.

STUFFED FIGS

At one of our grilling competitions, we had to grill fruit. To be different, we tried these stuffed figs.
I must admit, I had never had figs before. They were great! The creaminess of the cheese,
the sweetness of the honey, the tartness of the vinegar and the saltiness of the prosciutto
all blended in a delicious fig. They are great as appetizers.

MAKES ABOUT 8 SERVINGS

---

3 tbsp (45 ml) honey

1 tbsp (15 ml) balsamic vinegar

20 fresh figs

¼ cup (60 ml) mascarpone cheese

¼ cup (60 ml) blue cheese

1 tbsp (7 g) freshly ground black pepper

½ lb (225 g) prosciutto, paper thin

Set the Egg for 350°F (180°C) indirect. With the top and bottom vents wide open, light the fire and close the Egg. When the Egg gets up to about 250°F (121°C) dome, about 10 minutes, close the bottom screen. When the Egg approaches 350°F (180°C) dome, about 10 minutes, slide the top of the daisy wheel partially closed, leaving it a quarter of the way open.

In a small bowl, mix the honey and the vinegar together. Starting at the stem end, cut the figs down the middle, but not all the way through the bottom. Leave the bottom whole. Mix the mascarpone, blue cheese and the pepper together. Slice the prosciutto lengthwise into ¾-inch (18-mm) strips. Place a spoonful of the cheese mixture into each fig and wrap with a slice of prosciutto, being careful to wrap under the bottom and around all sides so the cheese won't melt out. Place the figs, bottom-side down onto the grate and grill until the prosciutto is browned, about 10 minutes. Remove from the Egg and drizzle with the honey-vinegar mixture and serve.

SWEET POTATO PIE

Sweet potato pie is known to be a Southern favorite. In the Northeast we see it made frequently over the holidays. It is sweet and savory and can be served as a side dish or a dessert.

MAKES 6 TO 8 SERVINGS

PIE CRUST

1¼ cups (156 g) all-purpose flour

1 tbsp (12 g) granulated sugar

¼ tsp salt

½ cup (120 ml) cold butter, diced

3 tbsp (45 ml) ice cold water

PIE FILLING

1½ lb (675 g) sweet potato, about 2 large

¾ cup (180 ml) heavy cream

½ cup (120 ml) butter, melted

½ cup (90 g) brown sugar, firmly packed

2 eggs, lightly beaten

¼ tsp table salt

1 tsp pure vanilla extract

½ tsp ground cinnamon

½ tsp ground nutmeg

Make the pie crust by mixing the flour, sugar and salt in a large bowl. Cut in the butter using a pastry blender or two knives until the mixture resembles pea-size crumbs. Add the ice water, 1 tablespoon (15 ml) at a time, tossing the dough with a fork to incorporate. Add enough of the water to bring the dough together. Gather the dough into a ball, and roll the dough on a lightly floured surface to a ⅛-inch (3-mm) thick, 12-inch (30-cm) circle. Transfer the dough to a deep-dish pie plate, trim and flute the edge and refrigerate until ready to fill.

Set the Egg up for 350°F (180°C) indirect with a raised rack. With the top and bottom vents wide open, light the fire and close the Egg. When the Egg gets up to about 250°F (121°C) dome, about 10 minutes, close the bottom screen. When the Egg approaches 350°F (180°C) dome, about 10 minutes, slide the top of the daisy wheel partially closed, leaving it a quarter of the way open. Wash the sweet potatoes, pierce with a fork, and place them on a piece of aluminum foil, on the grate, for 1 hour until tender.

Remove the potatoes from the Egg, and when cool enough to handle, cut in half and scoop the flesh into a large bowl. Mash with a potato masher until smooth, and then add the heavy cream, melted butter, brown sugar, eggs, salt, vanilla, cinnamon and nutmeg and mix well. Pour the mixture into the prepared crust, and place the pie on a raised rack in the Egg. Bake for 55 to 60 minutes, at 350°F (180°C), until a knife inserted in the center comes out clean. The pie will puff up like a soufflé but will sink down as it cools. Wait at least 1 hour before serving. Store in the refrigerator.

See photo on page 180.

HONEY MELON STEAKS

Fresh melon is always a good treat when grilling. Grilled melon is even better! Coating it with honey, salt and pepper will add a sweet and spicy accent to the slightly caramelized fruit. Growing up, I always put salt on melon. When I got older, I started adding pepper, too. It tastes even better! This melon can be served as a dessert or along with pork chops, fish or seafood. And you thought this was a steak recipe!

MAKES ABOUT 8 SERVINGS

1 large honeydew or cantaloupe melon

¼ cup (60 ml) honey

¼ cup (60 ml) lime juice,

½ tsp kosher salt

1 tbsp (7 g) freshly ground black pepper

Set the Egg for 350°F (180°C) direct. With the top and bottom vents wide open, light the fire and close the Egg. When the Egg gets up to about 250°F (121°C) dome, about 10 minutes, close the bottom screen. When the Egg approaches 350°F (180°C) dome, about 10 minutes, slide the top of the daisy wheel partially closed, leaving it a quarter of the way open.

Cut the melon in half and remove the seeds. Slice each half into ½-inch (13-mm) thick steaks. In a small bowl, mix the honey, lime juice, salt and pepper together. Clean the grate with an oiled cloth or a paper towel. When the Egg is up to temperature, lay the steaks on the grill and lightly brush the top side with the honey mixture, then flip and brush the honey on the second side. Grill for 2 minutes and then flip once more and grill for 1 more minute. The melon should be softened and have some charred grill marks. Do not over char. Remove the melon from the Egg and serve.

BACON CINNAMON ROLLS

Cinnamon rolls; I don't think they really need an introduction. Sweet, fluffy, sticky, spicy and gooey. However, we have added bacon and cayenne and made it a party no one will be late to!

MAKES ABOUT 15 SERVINGS

DOUGH

¼ oz (1 g) package active dry yeast

½ cup (120 ml) warm water

¼ cup (950 g) granulated sugar

½ cup (120 ml) milk

⅓ cup (80 ml) unsalted butter, melted

1 tsp kosher salt

1 large egg

3 to 3½ cups (375 to 437 g) all-purpose flour

FILLING

½ cup (120 ml) butter, melted

½ cup (100 g) brown sugar

2 tbsp (12 g) ground cinnamon

½ tsp cayenne pepper

8 slices applewood smoked bacon, partially cooked

GLAZE

3 tbsp (45 ml) unsalted butter, softened

1 cup (130 g) powdered sugar

½ tsp vanilla extract

3 tbsp (45 ml) milk

Dissolve the yeast in warm water and set aside. In the bowl of a stand mixer, with the paddle attachment, mix the sugar, milk, melted butter, salt and the egg. Add in 2 cups (250 g) of the flour and mix until smooth. Pour in the yeast mixture and combine. Mix in the remaining flour, ¼ cup (31 g) at a time, until the dough comes together and is easy to handle. If your dough looks dry, add water, a teaspoon at a time, mixing well after each addition. Switch to the dough hook and knead the dough for 6 to 8 minutes.

Place the dough in a well-oiled bowl and cover. Let rise in a warm place until doubled, for 1 to 1½ hours.

Punch down the dough and place it on a floured surface. Roll the dough out into a large rectangle, at least 15 inches (38 cm) long and 9 inches (23 cm) wide. In a small bowl, combine the melted butter, brown sugar, cinnamon and cayenne and spread it over the top of the dough. Add the sliced bacon evenly overtop. Starting at the longest side, roll the dough up into one long roll. Use a sharp knife to cut the roll into 1-inch (2.5-cm) pieces. Place the rolls in a lightly greased baking dish and cover, allowing them to rise for 45 minutes.

Set up the Egg for 350°F (180°C) indirect with a raised rack. With the top and bottom vents wide open, light the fire and close the Egg. When the Egg gets up to about 250°F (121°C) dome, about 10 minutes, close the bottom screen. When the Egg approaches 350°F (180°C) dome, about 10 minutes, slide the top of the daisy wheel closed, keeping the daisy wheel petals a quarter of the way open.

After the final rise, brush the raised cinnamon rolls with melted butter. When the Egg is up to temperature, bake for 25 to 30 minutes until golden.

Whisk glaze ingredients together until smooth and creamy. The mixture may look lumpy at first, but just continue to stir and it will come together. Add more milk, a teaspoon at a time, if a thinner consistency is desired.

Remove the cooked rolls from the Egg and pour the glaze overtop when rolls are slightly cooled. Serve warm.

DESSERT PIZZA

At many grilling competitions there is a pizza category. We tried the dessert pizza to be different and it was well received. The dough is a soft-baked cookie crust. When young children are present, you may want to cut back on the pepper jelly in the topping. It's a fun activity to involve the kids in, by letting them do the decorating of the finished pizza with their choice of fruits.

MAKES ABOUT 8 TO 10 SERVINGS

SUGAR COOKIE CRUST

½ cup (120 ml) unsalted butter, softened to room temperature

¾ cup (150 g) granulated sugar

1 large egg

1 tsp vanilla

1½ cups (190 g) all-purpose flour

¼ tsp salt

1 tsp baking powder

½ tsp baking soda

1½ tsp (5 g) cornstarch

TOPPING

2 tbsp (29 g) softened butter

8 oz (225 g) cream cheese, softened

1½ cups (195 g) confectioner's sugar

2 tbsp (30 ml) Texas Pepper Jelly® Strawberry Jalapeño

1 to 2 tbsp (15 to 30 ml) milk or cream

1 tsp vanilla

1 cup (154 g) fresh strawberries, sliced

1 cup (154 g) fresh blueberries

In a stand mixer, cream the softened butter on medium speed until smooth, about 1 minute. Add the sugar and then the egg and vanilla. In a separate bowl, whisk the flour, salt, baking powder, baking soda and cornstarch. With the mixer running at a low speed, slowly add these dry ingredients to the wet ingredients. Place dough in plastic wrap and refrigerate for at least 30 minutes.

Set the Egg for 350°F (180°C) indirect with a raised rack. With the top and bottom vents wide open, light the fire and close the Egg. When the Egg gets up to about 250°F (121°C) dome, about 10 minutes, close the bottom screen. When the Egg approaches 350°F (180°C) dome, about 10 minutes, slide the top of the daisy wheel partially closed, leaving it a quarter of the way open.

Remove the dough from the refrigerator and press onto a lightly greased 12-inch (30-cm) circular pizza pan. When the Egg is up to temperature, bake for 18 to 20 minutes, until the edges are very lightly browned. Remove from the Egg and let it cool on the pan for 10 to 15 minutes at room temperature, then place the crust in the refrigerator to finish cooling while you make the topping.

Beat the butter and the cream cheese together until smooth, about 2 minutes. Add the confectioner's sugar, the pepper jelly and 1 tablespoon (15 ml) of the milk, beating for 2 more minutes. Add the vanilla and 1 tablespoon (15 ml) of the milk, if needed, to thin out. Beat for another minute.

Spread all of the cream cheese mixture on the cooled cookie crust. Decorate with strawberries and blueberries or your choice of fruits just before serving, and slice with a pizza cutter or large chef's knife.

PUMPKIN STUFFED WITH BREAD PUDDING AND WHISKEY SAUCE

In this dessert, the stately pumpkin not only serves as a vessel for the bread pudding, but it creates a great presentation as well as giving a great fall flavor to the pudding. Pumpkin, pudding and whiskey sauce. Can it get any better?

MAKES 6 TO 8 SERVINGS

WHISKEY SAUCE

½ cup (120 ml) unsalted butter

½ cup (120 ml) heavy cream

½ cup (100 g) sugar

¼ cup (60 ml) bourbon

¼ cup (30 g) chopped walnuts

1 tsp vanilla extract

2 cups (480 ml) half-and-half

2 large eggs, beaten

¼ cup (57 g) brown sugar

2 tbsp (30 ml) maple syrup

½ tbsp (4 g) cinnamon

½ tbsp (7 ml) vanilla extract

2 cups (100 g) stale French bread, cut into ½-inch (1.3-cm) cubes

½ cup (120 g) Granny Smith apples, peeled, halved and sliced into 1-inch (2.5-cm) chunks

½ cup (600 g) dried cranberries

1 (3 lb [1.4 kg]) ripe pumpkin

¼ cup (57 g) butter, softened

For the whiskey sauce, in a medium saucepan on medium heat, melt the butter until it starts to turn light brown, about 5 minutes. Add the remaining sauce ingredients to the saucepan and bring to a simmer, stirring to dissolve the sugar. Cook for about 10 more minutes, until the sauce thickens, stirring frequently. When thickened, remove from the heat.

Set up the Egg for 350°F (180°C) dome indirect. With the top and bottom vents wide open, light the fire and close the Egg. When the Egg gets up to about 250°F (121°C) dome, about 10 minutes, close the bottom screen. When the Egg approaches 350°F (180°C) dome, about 10 minutes, slide the top of the daisy wheel partially closed, leaving it a quarter of the way open.

In a large bowl, stir together the half-and-half, eggs, brown sugar, maple syrup, cinnamon and vanilla to make custard. Add the cubed bread, apples and cranberries and gently combine.

Depending on the size of the pumpkin, you may need to make more stuffing. You can also stuff smaller sugar pumpkins for individual servings. Cut the top off of the pumpkin horizontally, about 2 inches (5 cm) down from the top. Remove the seeds and the pulp and discard. Rub the softened butter on the inside of the pumpkin, place the pumpkin into a pie plate and pour the stuffing mixture into the pumpkin.

When the Egg is up to 350°F (180°C) dome, bake the pumpkin for about 90 minutes, until the pudding is golden on top and firm in the center. Because of the eggs, it must reach at least 165°F (74°C) internal. The pumpkin should be soft when pricked with the tip of a knife.

To serve, place on the table center for presentation and spoon out servings of bread pudding and scrape a little cooked pumpkin flesh onto each dish and then drizzle with whiskey sauce. As an alternative, one which I prefer, cut a slice of the pumpkin to go with a spoonful of pudding, then drizzle with the sauce.

APPLE HAND PIES

Fruit hand pies, especially apple, are a Southern treat. These pies are deep-fried to create a crispy outside, with a warm and spicy inside. As an alternative, you can use any fresh fruit filling, such as strawberry, peach or blueberry. Stick a piece of cheddar cheese inside and you will be pleasantly surprised!

MAKES ABOUT 10 SERVINGS

1 tsp lemon juice

1 tbsp (15 ml) salted butter

2 cups (300 g) Granny Smith or other tart apple, peeled, cored and diced into ¼-inch (6-mm) pieces

1 tbsp (9 g) cornstarch

1½ cups (300 g) granulated sugar

½ tsp ground cinnamon

¼ tsp ground nutmeg

1 package of refrigerated pie dough, 2 sheets

1 qt (950 ml) vegetable oil for frying

¼ cup (32 g) powdered sugar

In a saucepan, combine the lemon juice, butter, apples, cornstarch, sugar, cinnamon and nutmeg. Simmer for about 15 minutes, stirring occasionally.

Set the Egg for 400°F (200°C) direct. With the top and bottom vents wide open, light the fire and close the Egg. When the Egg gets up to about 250°F (121°C) dome, about 10 minutes, close the bottom screen. When the Egg approaches 400°F (200°C) dome, about 10 to 12 minutes, slide the top of the daisy wheel partially closed, leaving it a quarter of the way open. Add the oil to a Dutch oven, about 2 inches (5 cm) deep, cover and heat on the Egg until the oil reaches 375°F (190°C).

While the oil is heating, cut the pie crust into 5-inch (13-cm) diameter circles and place 2 tablespoons (30 ml) of filling on the dough. Wet your finger in water and fold the dough in half. Press to seal. A dough press works well, but remember to wet the edges before pressing it closed. You can also use the tines of a fork to seal.

When the oil is hot, gently add 4 hand pies to the oil and fry, flipping once, for 5 or 6 minutes or until golden brown and crisp. Remove to a drying rack, dust with powdered sugar, and repeat until finished.

★ CHAPTER 10 ★
ABOUT THE EGG

PART I, TECHNIQUES FOR VARIOUS STYLES OF COOKING

ROASTING

When you think about roasting on a Big Green Egg, think of it as a brick oven with a smoke flavor component. In a conventional oven you can roast, but you will not add any subtle smoke flavor from the charcoal. You will also be roasting in a much drier environment than in the Egg. The Egg's moisture retention is far superior to a conventional oven's. This is accomplished without the use of a water pan. I never use water in the Egg. It's not necessary and will discourage the caramelization and crisping of the food you are cooking.

The setup for roasting is indirect, meaning that the heat is not directly below and exposed to the food. Indirect allows for more even cooking as opposed to grilling direct, where the underside of your roast is very hot and the top not as hot. You can grill many things direct, but it requires much more time and attention to flipping and turning, plus the Egg dome would be open more often. There is a saying in barbecue: If you are lookin', you ain't cookin'. By roasting indirect, the temperature stays more consistent and will allow the roast to cook more evenly.

An indirect cook is accomplished by placing a heat "shield" above the charcoal with a grid above it. The most popular "shield" is a Big Green Egg plate setter. It is placed on top of the fire ring, with the 3 legs pointing upward. You can put a foil-lined drip pan on the plate setter, then a grid on top of the plate setter legs for roasting. This would put the grid at about the same level as the dome gasket. If you don't have a plate setter, which I believe is the best and most often used accessory, you can use a pizza stone or your drip pan as a shield. For this, you would need one grid on top of the fire ring, and another above the drip pan. I have used bricks to support the second grate. I also use an indirect setup using accessories from the Ceramic Grill Store (www.thegrillstore.com), which work very well.

I mentioned placing your roast on the grid placed on the legs of your plate setter. For the best results, add an extended grid on top of this grid to make the roasting environment centered "up in the dome." You want to have everything in your Egg centered, including the roast, so the heat will come up evenly around the shield, then up and around and under the roast up in the dome. If you roast just on the grid resting on the plate setter legs, there will be less heat on the underside of the roast and more heat on top. However, if you are roasting several things at a time, using all grid levels is necessary. With any setup, however, you need to remember to rotate and flip a few times. There is a natural hot spot in the rear of the Egg. I always put one leg of the plate setter in the rear to mitigate the hotter temperature there. If you are roasting big and small items, the larger items should go to the rear of the Egg.

When I cook indirect, I always use a drip pan lined with foil on the plate setter. This will catch drippings and melted fat. Cleanup is easy, as you can throw the foil away after the cook. The drip pan will be dirty and will never be used for baking again, but by adding new foil before your next indirect cook, it will last forever. If you don't have a drip pan, you can make a foil drip pan by curling up the sides of the foil. Be careful! If you have a lot of grease and fat, it might leak onto the charcoal and cause a grease fire. If this happens, close the dome and the top and bottom vents and wait a few minutes before burping and opening the Egg to look inside. When you are done cooking, you can also leave the drip pan and the used foil in the Egg until it has cooled down, avoiding any possibility of spilling grease on the fire.

I generally start the Egg the same way for all cooks. This is discussed later in this chapter, where I describe when to add wood chunks or chips, and at what temperature to add the plate setter, drip pan, grid and your roast. The Egg is very easy to use. It takes only a little practice and minimal patience to learn what to do when and how to improvise, if necessary. The biggest factor, which comes naturally, is passion. We wouldn't be Eggheads if we didn't have great passion for cooking on the Egg!

BARBECUE

Barbecue is often called low and slow—low temperatures over a long period of cook time. Temperatures usually range between 200°F and 275°F (93°C and 140°C). Grilling, on the other hand, is hotter and faster, higher temperatures for a shorter period of time. Barbecue is not only about the low and slow cooking method but also the social gathering that surrounds cooking outdoors and feeding many hungry and chatty people! Often, most barbecues are grilling meat hot and fast, not low and slow. It doesn't matter the method; it is still a barbecue. You wouldn't call it a "grilling," would you? That only happens when you stay out way too late or you've been invited down to the station. Grillings aren't pleasant.

Most barbecue meats are cheap because they are tough. They are the opposite of tenderloin. The best way to get the barbecue meats tender is to cook them at a low temperature for a long time, so the outside doesn't burn before the center is tender. Big meats, like beef brisket, beef or pork ribs and pork shoulder, take a long time for the collagen and connective tissues to dissolve and for the meat to become tender. The flavor was always there, but if it wasn't tender, your teeth, jaw bone and tongue would get all worn out before you could taste anything. Many of the large cuts are ground into hamburger or sausage. Barbecue, however, changes everything.

The process is really fairly simple. Build a fire, add wood chunks for smoke flavor, rub the meat with a flavorful dry rub, cook indirect at a low temperature and wait! The wait may be the only hard part. Before I started competition barbecue, I cooked my pork butts for 20 to 22 hours, at about 200°F (93°C) on 1 load of lump. The irresistible smell of the meat cooking would penetrate the neighborhood. Walk around at a barbecue competition at 5 a.m. and the aromas are heavenly! At the Greenfield, Massachusetts, competition, I met a police officer who had just gone off duty at 7 a.m., and when he opened the station door a half mile away from the competition site, he smelled the barbecue. He was from the South and followed his nose right to the competition!

Barbecue is cooked indirect with a drip pan in the Egg. The setup is the same as for roasting, except the dome temperature is in the range of 225°F to 275°F (107°C to 140°C), depending on the meat, and the cook is longer. Pork butt and beef brisket can cook at 250°F (121°C) dome for about 10 hours, depending on their size and if you foil the meat, which I will discuss next. Ribs can cook at 250°F (121°C) dome for 4 to 5 hours, depending also on the size of the racks and if you foil.

I mentioned earlier that I used to cook pork butts for over 20 hours. They came out great! With competition, however, I don't have the luxury of time and will cook at a higher temperature and will use foil to speed up the cook time. Some purists refer to wrapping in foil as "the Texas crutch." Crutch or not, I find that foiling will yield outstanding results and most competition cooks use it. The meat will be cooked at 160°F (71°C), but won't be tender until it reaches 190°F to 200°F (88°C to 93°C). After the meat reaches about 160°F (71°C), the meat's internal temperature will stall or plateau at this temperature for hours until all the collagen and connective tissue has dissolved. The internal temperature rises ever so slowly, but the meat is still cooking and going through a physical change, which takes time. Foiling will speed up the process, and I believe, as do the judges, it can give perfect results. When I foil, I double wrap the meat in foil and add a little liquid before sealing up the foil and returning the meat to the Egg. I use a beef flavored stock for beef and fruit juice for pork.

For all indirect cooks, I use the dome temperature. The dome temperature in the Egg for an indirect can be 15°F to 30°F (9°C to 18°C) more than the grid temperature because of the way the heat circulates around the plate setter and up past the grid into the dome. The longer the cook, the less the differential. A low and slow cook will be at a lower temperature for a long time and the grid temperature will rise to close to the dome temperature. I use the dome temperature because that is where the thermometer is, and I don't need to open the Egg to temp the grid or add a probe.

Checking the grid temperature is one extra step I personally do not use. The dome temperature reference works well. Why keep track of two temperatures when one will do? This is analogous to only controlling the Egg temperature with the daisy wheel top vent, leaving the bottom vent open and screened.

After about an hour, the brisket, pork or ribs should reach about 190°F to 200°F (88°C to 93°C), and past the plateau. At this point I wrap the foiled pork and brisket in a towel and place it in an empty cooler to rest for several hours, and at least 1 hour. The ribs don't need to rest and can be unwrapped and placed back on the Egg at 300°F to 350°F (149°C to 177°C) dome for about half an hour. Sauce, if desired, is added in the last 10 to 15 minutes to glaze the ribs. The same applies for the brisket flat, but make sure to reserve the broth from the foil for dipping. When adding sauce, do not have the temperature higher than 350°F (177°C) dome to prevent the sugar in the sauce from burning.

The pork shoulder can be taken out of the foil and pulled, chopped or sliced, with some of the broth from the foil added as well as a little sauce. The recipes that follow give more specific directions for barbecuing different cuts of meat.

GRILLING

The Big Green Egg is very well suited for grilling. As mentioned above, grilling is done at higher temperatures for a shorter period of time than barbecue. Searing temperatures on the Egg can be 450°F (230°C) and up to 750°F (399°C). This is accomplished direct, and sometimes direct to sear, then indirect to finish (roast). The key is to create a flavorful crust on the outside while letting the inside cook to the desired doneness, usually medium rare for me. If you cook at too high of a temperature, you can cook the outside before the inside is done cooking or overcook the inside. At too low a temperature, you could have the inside cooked before the outside has the "perfect sear."

A few key words of advice are to have your grid well oiled and clean before searing. When the grid is hot, you can use tongs and paper towel splashed with vegetable oil to rub down the grid. My preference is to use a cast iron grid for searing. Each bar of the grid is super-heated and will sear and leave tasty grill marks. It also needs to be oiled, or well seasoned. Once you put your meat on, don't move it until it is time to turn. It should "release" from the grid when the grill marks have cooked. Also, only use tongs or spatulas to move the meat. Never use a carving fork! That will release invaluable juices needlessly! Speaking of juices, searing does not sear in the juices, no way, no how. The juices are only retained by your control of the temperature and timing of the cook. By following these steps, you will have juicy and tender bites every time. Also, don't press burgers down on the grate. That will only push the juices out and make them dry. Always let your grilled meat rest on a grid under tented foil for 10 to 15 minutes. This gives time for the juices to redistribute and is a must for juicy meat!

Some recipes call for searing then roasting indirect to finish. If you are cooking direct and your fire gets too hot, or the meat is searing too quickly before the inside is cooked, you can always remove the meat from the Egg, close the vents and let it cool down. If the outside temperature is 70°F (21°C) or lower, a 750°F (399°C) dome Egg can cool down to about 400°F (204°C) dome in about 20 minutes if both the top and bottom vents are closed. If it is hotter outside, it is more difficult to cool the Egg down. When it is hot outside, it is best to sneak up on your searing temperature slowly and don't over shoot it, the key is not to let the fire get too hot and intense. Consider searing at 450°F (232°C) dome if you need to get the Egg to a lower temperature thereafter. You can also plan to sear after you have cooked other foods at a lower temperature. A patio umbrella will also keep the Egg in the shade. (And you, too!) You can also fill the fire box up one-quarter to one-third of the way before lighting. Less charcoal to start with will die down quicker than a full firebox. As a last resort, you can place the hot coals in a small, covered metal garbage can on a noncombustible surface. I use one for all my ash when cleaning out my Eggs. With limited lit charcoal, you can leave the dome open to cool off the Egg. Do not put water in the Egg. It can crack it or get into the porcelain and freeze and cause problems with the fire. All of this may sound complicated or cumbersome, but it really isn't. It is like driving a car. You don't always consciously put on your brake or step on the gas, but you stop and go just fine when necessary.

One huge word of caution: always be prepared for flash back, especially when opening an Egg that was very hot when the dome was closed. See the section on safety in part III (page 208) in this chapter.

BAKING

The Big Green Egg is a great ceramic oven. It retains heat and moisture very well. Baking is done indirect, as with roasting. Temperature and time will be similar to your kitchen oven's. You can use similar racks, baking sheets, casserole dishes or cast-iron cookware as you do in your home oven. There are a few remarkable differences between your oven and the Big Green Egg. First, you can bake all day and never overheat your kitchen. Second, there will be more moisture retained when baking on the Egg. Third, a little hint of smoky flavor from the lump charcoal adds an earthy note to your baked goods. Last, when was the last time you had a pizza party and baked pizza after pizza at 600°F (315°C) in your kitchen?

Just as with roasting, baking is best up in the dome for uniform cooking. You can bake indirect at the grid level, but it is better to cook on a raised grid above the grid level. This allows for more even heat circulation under and around your baked food up in the dome. Remember to rotate the food at least once during your cook to compensate for hot spots. Baking in multiple layers within the Egg works well, provided you move and rotate as well.

HOT AND COLD SMOKING

The more you use the Big Green Egg, the more you'll want to try new things. Smoking cured meat is one of those ways. Curing meat is accomplished by applying either dry or wet curing methods. Dry curing is the application of a dry rub containing curing agents, applied to the raw meat surface. The meat is wrapped in plastic wrap, vacuum sealed or put into large resealable plastic bags and refrigerated for several days, turned and massaged daily. Wet curing is the process of submerging the meat in a refrigerated brine containing curing agents for several days.

When cured, the meat can be refrigerated or frozen until ready to cook. Alternately, it can be smoked to add flavor, and if desired, smoked to an internal temperature of fully cooked meat. There are many ways to cure and smoke. Cold smoking is done so that the meat or cheese smokes for a few hours but never reaches an internal temperature over 100°F (38°C). Cold smoked meat is not fully cooked and needs to be refrigerated or frozen until ready to cook. Hot smoking will smoke the meat for several hours at a higher temperature until the internal temperature reaches about 160°F (71°C). At this time, the cured meat is fully cooked.

The setup I use for hot smoking is a fire box only one-quarter to one-third full of charcoal. The smaller pile of lump will provide less fire and heat. I put wood chunks on the lit coals and the meat is cooked up in the dome on a raised grid, indirect with a drip pan. The desired dome temperature is 200°F (93°C) or less.

The setup I use for cold smoking utilizes an empty fire box and the A-Maze-N Pellet smoker, which is a perforated maze that holds smoking food grade pellets. I want to keep the meat or cheese temperature below 90°F (32°C) internal, so I use only smoke, no charcoal. I set up the Egg direct because there is no flame and I want the smoke to circulate around all the meat or cheese.

DEEP-FRYING, GRIDDLING AND WOK-ING AROUND—OTHER GREAT WAYS TO COOK ON THE BIG GREEN EGG.

The Big Green Egg is the Ultimate Cooking Experience™ and also the most versatile cooking appliance. Sure, you can wok and deep-fry in the kitchen. You remember how good the food tasted. You will also be reminded for days that you smelled up the house with fried oil, garlic and fish! Cook it all on the Egg and you won't heat up the house or stink it up for days!

Using a Dutch oven on the Egg is the perfect way to deep-fry. It stays hot and helps the oil recover faster if the temperature drops. It is much safer than using a frying-pan to shallow fry in, which I would not recommend. However, a Dutch oven has a bale handle, a lid, and is deep enough to make deep-frying safe and efficient. Always add oil to the Dutch oven when it is off the Egg, and never fill more than 2½ inches (6 cm) from the top. Oil in a covered Dutch oven can heat up to the desired temperature (325°F to 375°F [160°C to 190°C]) while the Egg is coming up to temperature. As long as the lid is on the Dutch oven when the dome is closed, there will never be a problem with the oil catching fire. (If it ever did, put the lid back on the Dutch oven, close the dome and vents until the fire snuffs out. I have never had this happen, however.) If the oil gets too hot, cover it and take it off the Egg, then remove the lid from it to cool the oil.

The Big Green Egg is perfect for using a wok as well. The wok temperature should be up to about 450°F (230°C), and the Egg has no difficulty doing that! The wok sits right on the grid, direct. All you need is a pair of welder's gloves to handle the wok. Wok cooking is quick, so make sure you have all your ingredients measured and available before starting. If your wok has a rounded bottom, make sure you have a wok stand or a large pot handy to keep the wok upright when you remove it from the Egg.

I have always loved Chinese food but never attempted to cook it until I got my first Egg. It's easy and the food is fantastic!

Fried food, outdoors with friends and family, is like you are at the fair and never had to pay admission!

PART II, THE BIG GREEN EGG CONSTRUCTION, COMPONENTS, ACCESSORIES AND USING RUBS, SAUCES AND OTHER KITCHEN ACCESSORIES

CONSTRUCTION AND COMPONENTS

Regardless of the size of the Big Green Egg, they are all set up the same. From the outside there is the bottom with the lower vent. The top of the Egg is called the dome and has an upper vent. For the upper vent opening, there is a ceramic rain cap that should be put on the Egg to snuff out the fire, along with closing the lower vent. The rain cap should be placed on the Egg when not in use.

Between the dome and the bottom, there is a gasket, which helps keep a seal. A hinge assembly, attached to the bottom of the dome, helps the dome stay open when raised, and keeps the bottom and the dome aligned properly. The seal is important for long cooks, where the fire is fed by fresh air being drafted from the bottom vent up through the charcoal, and then the heat and smoke are drafted up and out the top vent. If the seal is not good, the heat will be drafted through the gasket openings and the dome temperature will not be as high as it should be. For a long cook, this could cause the lump to burn out at a much higher temperature than desired, and the lump could run out before the meat is cooked. In essence, the heat bypasses the meat and goes out the gasket gaps.

For faster cooks, it is not as important to have a tight fit because the top vent is opened more. There are a few common reasons for the gasket to fail. When the Egg is new, the cement holding the gasket may or may not have set well enough and should be recemented. You should not do a high-temperature cook the first few times you use your new Egg. Flash back can start to burn the gasket. I don't use my plate setter with the legs down because the heat and possible flash back are directed right at the level of the gasket. Air may also be escaping because the top and bottom hinges do not align the Egg bottom and dome and the hinges need to be adjusted. I own half a dozen Eggs, and since 2000 have never replaced a gasket. That doesn't mean that they haven't been burned or aren't worn out. When it is important for a long cook to have the gasket sealed, I will fold a piece of aluminum foil 3 or 4 times to a width of about 1 inch (2.5 cm), then cover the curvature of the gasket by inserting a piece long enough to create a seal when closed. It works for me! Having a good gasket, however, may help prevent chipping of the Egg if it is inadvertently dropped shut.

Inserted in the inside of the bottom is the fire ring. It holds the burning charcoal. It has a mouse hole in the bottom side, which needs to align with the bottom vent for the Egg to draft properly. A cast-iron fire grate sits in the fire ring near the bottom and allows air to draft up through its holes into the charcoal. The side of the firebox also has nickel-sized holes to allow air to draft into the charcoal from the sides. Make sure they are not plugged with ash.

The fire ring sits inside the Egg on top of the fire box. The purpose is to create a void area in which the charcoal can burn. Usually the charcoal is put into the fire box up to the bottom of the fire ring. Too much higher and the combustion chamber area for the charcoal would be limited and would prevent even burning, causing it to die out or not get as hot. Both the fire box and the fire ring create an interior lining for the Egg where it gets the hottest. Do not use the Egg without the fire ring and fire box in place.

Next, on top of the fire ring, sits either a grid for direct cooking or a plate setter for indirect cooking. For direct cooking, I prefer to use a well-seasoned cast-iron grate. It retains the heat when cold meat is placed on it, and the bars retain the heat that sears the grill marks. Grill marks tell me that the meat was seared and will taste better. I don't doubt, however, that you could go to a chain restaurant where they paint the grill marks on with food coloring, and all the patrons would go gaga!

When using a plate setter on top, I always use it with the legs up and a grid underneath. The extra grid helps catch anything that may have rolled off the upper grid and gives me the peace of mind that, Heaven forbid, if the plate setter fails my food won't end up in the fire. However, when you set up the plate setter, always put on a leg in the rear of the Egg because that is where the draft is hottest.

Once you have set up on the top of the fire box, you have many choices for setups. In this book I explain my set up for each recipe. You will see the common factors. I always use a foil lined drip pan on the plate setter when cooking indirect. I hate getting the plate setter cruddy, and some of that fat and liquid can burn when dripped and create an acidy smoke. Unless I am doing a multi-level cook, I prefer to cook "up in the dome" on a raised rack on top of the bottom grid. This allows for more even cooking around the food. My preferred pizza or baking setup is a plate setter, legs up, grid on top of the legs, a raised grid on top of the bottom grid and a pizza stone on the raised grid.

ACCESSORIES

There are numerous accessories for the Egg, for griddles and for multilevel cooking. Some are half-moon shaped, so you can cook at different levels using different techniques.

The Ceramic Grill Store also has many accessories for the Egg, including multilevel grid systems for cooking higher in the dome, as well as down below the bottom of the fire ring for indirect cooking. They also carry woks and other accessories that I find very useful in addition to Big Green Egg accessories.

Once you have the basics down on using your Egg, you will enjoy learning and creating techniques that suit you best. The Egg is your canvas; you have the brushes, now go paint something delicious!

RUBS AND SAUCES

Dry rubs are essential to great-tasting smoked, roasted and grilled meats and vegetables. You can make your own or select from many in-store and online sources. The best selection of multiflavored rubs and seasonings come from Dizzy Pig. They are a longtime Championship barbecue team using Big Green Eggs, and besides creating excellent rubs, they are a Big Green Egg dealer. You can get their products online, in store, or check the dealer locations. If your Big Green Egg dealer doesn't already carry them, ask them to. They are the best!

You can also make your own rubs. There are many recipes available online, and once you get started, you may enjoy creating your own recipes. A few tips are to use turbinado sugar because of its higher burning point, and be careful of the amount of salt you use. Whether you make your own or get them commercially, remember that they have a shelf life. After a period of months, and certainly after a year, most herbs and spices lose their flavor and all you are left with is salt. I used to make my own rubs, but it is much easier for me to buy them commercially and blend them together if necessary.

BASIC BEEF RUB

MAKES ABOUT 1 CUP (160 G)

½ cup (56 g) paprika

3 tbsp (54 g) kosher salt

3 tbsp (10 g) freshly ground black pepper

2 tbsp (18 g) garlic powder

2 tbsp (18 g) onion powder

2 tsp (4 g) cayenne pepper

Mix all ingredients together and store in an airtight container for up to 3 months.

BASIC PORK RUB

MAKES ABOUT 1½ CUPS (240 G)

¼ cup (28 g) sweet paprika

½ cup (152 g) turbinado sugar

3 tbsp (54 g) kosher salt

2 tbsp (6 g) freshly ground black pepper

2 tbsp (16 g) chili powder

2 tbsp (18 g) onion powder

2 tbsp (18 g) ground mustard

1 tsp cayenne pepper

Mix all ingredients together and store in an airtight container for up to 3 months.

BASIC POULTRY RUB

MAKES ABOUT 1 CUP (160 G)

2 tbsp (14 g) sweet paprika

¼ cup (76 g) turbinado sugar

1½ tbsp (27 g) kosher salt

1 tbsp (3 g) freshly ground black pepper

1 tbsp (8 g) chili powder

1 tbsp (9 g) garlic powder

1 tbsp (9 g) onion powder

1 tbsp (9 g) ground mustard

½ tsp cayenne pepper

1 tsp dried oregano

1 tsp dried rosemary

1 tsp dried thyme

Mix all ingredients together and store in an airtight container for up to 3 months.

The type of sauce you like and use is often based on where you live. Sauces can be vinegar, mustard, tomato or even mayonnaise based. I think Sweet Baby Ray's® sauce is good on pork and chicken and Cattleman's® is good on beef. Online, check out the Slabs for sauces and rubs. For competition, I often use sauce from Slabs. Personally, I prefer my barbecue dry, and I prefer sauce on the side.

Many of the recipes have ingredients that can be substituted for another ingredient. I often use maple syrup, but you can substitute molasses or honey if you desire. If you like more heat, you can add more cayenne pepper. What you decide to use for rubs and sauces can be determined by personal preference.

OTHER KITCHEN ACCESSORIES

Additional kitchen accessories I find useful are a vacuum tumbler for marinating and a vacuum sealer for marinades and for freezing fresh and leftover meats. If you chop up your cooked pork or brisket and add a little sauce, it can be vacuum sealed and frozen. To serve, just reheat the bag of meat in boiling water or the microwave. Barbecue often tastes better the next day, and if frozen, it can be eaten whenever you get the urge!

PART III SAFETY, LIGHTING, TEMPERATURE CONTROL, SMOKE AND MAINTENANCE

Learning to cook on the Big Green Egg includes learning procedures to keep you from getting burned, as well as food-safety procedures. Using the Egg is not dangerous, but it does contain an open flame when open. Just like you need to be careful around your fireplace or woodstove, you need to be careful around your Egg. For starters, I always use leather welder's gloves to open the Egg and to handle all the tools, accessories and components. I buy them at a local discount store for $6, and when they get too stiff to use, I buy another pair.

The number one concern for Egg safety is planning for and avoiding flash back. Flash back happens when the Egg dome is opened and fresh oxygen becomes available to the charcoal and explodes into a ball of fire. The most common time for flash back is when you have a hot fire and close the Egg vents down, which helps lower the temperature but also starves the fire for air. If you open the dome too soon, flash back can occur. To combat flash back, wear gloves when opening the Egg, and always burp it. Burping means slowly lifting the dome about 3 inches (7.5 cm), waiting a couple of seconds, and then slowly opening all the way. Burping allows a smaller amount of air to reach the charcoal, which will create flames, but not enough to allow too much air all at once, creating a fireball. I habitually always burp the Egg, but I sometimes forget when I am distracted or gabbing. Don't let anyone who doesn't know about burping the Egg open it, or they might get a frightening crash course in flash back. Flash back is less likely to occur when the Egg is below 300°F (150°C), but it can still happen, especially after the plate setter is first added and the fire has not settled down yet.

Be aware that when you have a hot fire and add big meats and close down the vents, the draft can immediately reverse and flames can shoot out the bottom vent. Even with the screen closed, flames can still cough out the bottom. You must always use the bottom vent screen. Not just flames, but embers can be shot out. Just ask Chris Capell from Dizzy Pig, who had a devastating house fire when embers blew into his garage. After that, Big Green Egg developed the bottom screen for the Eggs. I will only have the screen open when starting the Egg to allow for more air flow to create the draft. As soon as I know the Egg is heating up on its own, I will close the screen.

Always use a drip-pan when flammable fat is rendering. Make sure the pan is deep enough to hold the grease. Flash back can catch the drip-pan grease on fire. Even when grilling with a drip pan, sometimes flames can reach up into the drip pan and catch it on fire. If you have a fire, close the dome and all of the vents to starve the flames. Beware of flash back when you reopen the dome. If necessary, carefully remove the grease during your cook if it is getting too deep in your drip pan. Do not use a disposable aluminum pan for a drip pan, as it might melt.

In your cooking area, keep a heat resistant spot where you can place a hot grid or plate setter from the Egg either to cool it down or while rearranging the inside of the Egg. Always have gloves readily available.

For food safety, I always use an instant-read thermometer. Thermopen from Thermo Works is my favorite. I keep one at home, one in the competition trailer and one at the lake house. You can use dial thermometers, but the instant read keeps my hand from getting too hot and keeps the dome open very briefly. You can use the touch method, but I rely on the Thermapen to tell me that my food is cooked before serving it to family, friends or the judges.

Safe serving temperatures after resting are 165°F (74°C) for ground turkey, chicken and other poultry; 160°F (71°C) for ground beef or pork; 145°F (63°C) for beef steaks, pork chops, fresh pork and ham and seafood.

When checking the temperature, especially with poultry, check it in several areas, especially in the thickest part.

Keep cooked food above 140°F (60°C). It must be cooled to 41°F (5°C) within 4 hours to be safe. If reheating, heat to at least 165°F (74°C).

I always use powder-free latex gloves when handling raw or cooked meat. If you wash your hands well and often, raw meat can be handled without gloves before it's cooked. I just can't! I am not a clean freak, but I always wear gloves. Gloves should be changed often. Dirty gloves are as bad as dirty hands.

Also be aware of cross-contamination. Raw chicken should never be stored above other foods. Do not let raw chicken in your ice cooler sink into the ice water. When cutting chicken, never reuse cutting boards or utensils without washing and sanitizing them. That includes changing your gloves.

Raw meat and fish should smell clean. When they smell bad, you know they're bad. One exception, however, would be large cuts like beef brisket, pork butts and especially pork ribs. They can have an off-smell when removed from the cryovac. This can be caused by physical changes while being vacuum sealed and is not necessarily spoilage. Rinse the meat thoroughly under cold water. If the smell is gone, you are all set. When in doubt, throw it out!

LIGHTING THE BIG GREEN EGG

First, and very important, NEVER use lighter fluid in the Egg! It can get soaked up in the pores of the ceramic and will never come out! The smell and the taste will last and last. Also, beware if you are looking to buy a used Egg. It may have been ruined by lighter fluid.

Before lighting your Egg, stir any leftover lump around to let ash settle to and through the bottom fire grate. You can use a large, perforated metal spoon. I use an ice fishing ice skimmer. The Egg ash tool can also be used to stir up the leftover lump. Check periodically to see if any of the vent holes in the side of the fire box are clogged, and clean them out. Open the bottom vent all the way and rake the ash out into a metal bucket. Make sure that the mouse hole in the bottom side of the fire box lines up with the vent opening and is not off center.

Dump the lump into the Egg, up to the top of the fire box at the bottom of the fire ring. If you are planning to do an overnight cook, you can load maybe an inch higher but no more than that. You need to leave room for air to get in and circulate and draft properly.

To start the charcoal, fire starters will work as well as electric gadgets. Some people use a chimney charcoal starter and light it in the Egg, then dump the hot, burning lump into the Egg. I prefer to light the lump in the fire box. It is less messy. For years, I have used a Mapp gas handheld torch. It is hotter than propane and it is what plumbers use to solder copper pipes. I make three "divots" in a triangular pattern in the charcoal. One is always in the rear. The torch has a self-lighter and can be set to stay burning without holding the button down. I hold it in each divot for a minute or so before going on to the next divot. The more you continue, the shorter the time to hold the torch in each spot. If the torch goes out while you are holding it in place, it's a good thing. It means the fire is getting hot and there is a lack of oxygen to keep it going. When a flame remains in the charcoal for a few seconds after you remove the torch, close the lid and keep the daisy wheel all the way open. The Egg should be up to 300°F (150°C) dome in about 10 minutes. If you need to, you can burp the Egg and hit each spot with the torch again.

The temperature you are shooting for to start the Egg is decided by a few factors. You first want to make sure that your fire is going in the three areas before continuing. If you put your food on and the fire hasn't spread out enough, it might die, especially during a long cook. The entire lump doesn't need to be lit, just three spots. Close the screen all the way on the bottom vent. Leave the bottom vent door open all the way. When the Egg reaches the desired dome temperature and you are cooking a long cook, add the wood chunks to the charcoal. Add the plate setter, feet up, with one leg in the rear. Add the drip pan, then the grid. Close the dome, but keep the daisy wheel wide open until the Egg comes back up to your desired cooking temperature, then close and adjust it. Let the smoke settle down to a bluish-gray color, then add your meat. With a big piece of meat, the temperature may drop again. You can open up the daisy wheel and then reset it when the Egg comes back up to the desired temperature, providing the smoke does not get too heavy.

If it isn't very warm out, say 75°F (24°C), and you are not adding wood chunks or chips, you can overshoot the desired cooking temperature by 25° to 50°F (15° to 30°C) before adding the plate setter, drip pan and grid. When you close the dome, the temperature will drop back near your desired temperature. Adjust the daisy wheel to the desired amount, and add your food to the Egg when the temperature has climbed back up to the desired dome temperature. If it is hotter than 75°F (24°C) more than you want it, sneak up to your desired temperature and do not overshoot before putting in the plate setter, drip pan and grid. Adjust the vent to the desired temperature, and when corrected, add the food.

Alternative ways to start the Egg are food-grade paraffin fire starters or an electric fire starter. You'll still light in three spots in a triangle as described above. Old-school pit masters can also use a charcoal chimney starter. Load the unlit lump in the fire box and fill up the chimney. Place the grid on the Egg. Stuff the bottom of the chimney with newspaper and light, setting it on the grid when lit. When the charcoal in the chimney is well lit, remove the grid and dump it into the fire box.

TEMPERATURE CONTROL

Temperature control on the Big Green Egg works just like a woodstove or a fireplace. Air comes into the fire and is controlled by a damper above the fire. Open it and the fire gets hotter; close it and the fire subsides. On the Egg, air comes in through the bottom vent, through the burning charcoal, and then up into the dome and out the top vent. I control the temperature by opening and closing the daisy wheel on the top vent. I leave the bottom vent wide open with the screen closed. I was instructed a long time ago to adjust both the top vent and the bottom vent so that each has the same amount of opening. After many long cooks, and going up and down the stairs all night to adjust each vent to keep at my desired cooking temperature, I abandoned that theory and now only adjust the daisy wheel, leaving the bottom open all the way with the screen closed.

Cindi and I spend a lot of money competing, and cooking well is extremely important. For longer cooks, once the Egg has settled down at my desired temperature (I wait about an hour), I set the daisy wheel one last time and go to bed without the worry that my competition meats may not cook correctly. I wouldn't do it this way if it wasn't reliable.

Eggs of every size function the same. The time it takes to heat up, however, is different, depending on the size. The medium comes up to temperature faster than the large, and the large faster than the extra large. The more mass to heat up, the longer it takes. There is not a big difference, but it is real.

The dual function daisy wheel is wide open until the desired temperature is reached. In this chapter, under "Lighting the Big Green Egg," *when* to adjust the daisy wheel temperature is discussed. Now, I'll discuss how to adjust the daisy wheel to get the desired temperature.

First, the dual function daisy wheel slides open for maximum draft and highest temperatures. The place that slides open also spins on itself and can allow its oval-shaped openings, or daisy petals, to be closed, partially opened, or opened all the way. When the top slides closed, the air amount is adjusted by the amount of opening by the petal size. These adjustments are for lower temperatures.

Petals all open	300°F (150°C)
Petals half open	250°F to 275°F (120°C to 140°C)
Petals one-quarter open	225°F (107°C)
Petals slightly open	190°F to 200°F (88°C to 93°C)

Not all of the petal holes may be perfectly shaped or line up perfectly, so use the average. You can also tighten or loosen the nuts on the daisy wheel to make the adjustments easier or harder.

If you are looking to cook at higher temperatures, you can slide the top open to permit more airflow. When sliding the top open, the petal openings don't matter.

Slide one-quarter open	325°F to 400°F (160°C to 200°C)
Slide half open	425°F to 550°F (220°C to 288°C)
Slide three-quarters open	575°F to 700°F (302°C to 371°C)
Slide all the way open	725°F and above (385°C and above)

Holding temperatures below 375°F (190°C) are easier to accomplish than higher temperatures. When you slide the top open, the temperature will rise quickly. Once the charcoal has more oxygen with a larger draft, it can really take off. Higher temperature settings should be monitored more closely than when using the daisy wheel slide closed and with the petals open.

Increasing the temperature in the Egg is easier than lowering it. This is due to the ceramic's getting hot, and as a great insulator, it cools very slowly. The fire can be reduced by closing down the vents, but the dome temperature may stay hot for a long time. If you are planning a cook, try to cook your high temperature cooks last, or spread out the cooks of individual foods, giving the Egg time to cool down. You can reasonably get the Egg down from 700°F (371°C) to 400°F (200°C) by closing the top and the bottom vents and maybe putting the rain cap on until the temperature drops near your desired setting. If the outside temperature is 70°F (21°C) or below, this could take between 20 and 30 minutes. If the temperature is above 80°F (27°C), it will take much longer. Be extremely cautious of flash back when you are reducing the temperature. The dome temperature may be coming down, but if you open the Egg, the fire, which is still very hot and starved for oxygen, can easily erupt. Wear heat-resistant gloves and burp the Egg slower and longer than normal.

I always refer to dome temperature with my recipes. I am used to it, and that is where the thermometer is located. For indirect cooks, grid level temperature will usually be less than the dome temperature. I take this into account when I am cooking a multilevel cook. Food at the grid level will cook slower than food up in the dome. I move food around as necessary. Rotation is important because of possible hot spots and colder zones due to how the food is stacked or how the fire is drafting.

The dome temperature may drop when you add the plate setter and large meats, especially in a low and slow cook. The temperature will come back up in a few minutes. If it doesn't, open the top vent to provide more air flow and draft until you get back to your cooking temperature, then reset the daisy wheel.

Your dome thermometer should be calibrated regularly. Your Egg may be cooking hotter or colder all the time while you stand there scratching your head! Take the thermometer out of the dome and put a pair of pliers on the nut under the dial. Place at least 1 inch (2.5 cm) of the thermometer tip into boiling water and see if it reads 212°F (100°C). If not, hold the dial with a cloth and rotate it until it is at 212°F (100°C). It may take a couple of tries before you get it calibrated.

Many people use other temperature probes, electronic thermometers and fan temperature controls. I don't use extra thermometers anymore and have only tried the BBQ Guru once. I don't have a problem with them. If you want to have more proof or evidence of how your cook is going, it's your thing! If you want to sit inside and monitor the cook on your laptop, go ahead! It's a personal preference. They work very well. Setting the daisy wheel works well for me. Heck, there are some out there who say if you aren't cooking on a stick burner, then you can't cook barbecue. I beg to differ, guru or not!

There are environmental factors that affect temperature control on the Egg. If it is a very hot day, the Egg will cool down slower. If it is windy, with 20 mile-per-hour gusts, the draft can be interrupted or reversed. A wind gust may suck air out of the bottom vent or top vent. When it is this windy, I do close the bottom vent so that the opening is the same amount as the daisy wheel. If your charcoal is wet or has picked up moisture, it will not get as hot as you need it to, regardless of how much the vents are open. Either discard it, or dry it in the sun.

Two environmental factors that do not affect the Egg temperature are rain and cold. If your Egg is up to temperature, the superior insulation qualities of the Egg won't be hampered by rain or cold. You may be personally affected by the rain, but patio umbrellas or canopies solve that. When it is cold, remember to place a stick the size of a pencil between the dome and the bottom before you put the weather cover on your Egg at the end of your cook. The gasket will pick up moisture and will freeze shut. I know from experience, but a frozen Egg never kept me from cooking ribs on Super Bowl Sunday, especially when the Patriots were playing!

SMOKE

I like my food cooked on the Egg to be smoked but not smoky. The right amount of smoke should add a subtle flavor to the food. Too much smoke or, even worse, bad smoke will ruin a good cut of meat or fish. Have you ever prepared to put a bite of barbecued food in your mouth, and just before it hits your lips, your nose twitches, your tongue runs backward, you get ready to cough, and a slight tear comes to your eye? This is a case of too much smoke! If you still take a bite and the back of your throat painfully cracks and dries out, you had some bad smoke. Been there? It's just as bad as a burger from the hibachi, smelling and tasting like lighter fluid. YUCK!

The problem comes from using too strong of a smoke, combined with smoking too long and not letting the billowing smoke settle down to a bluish-gray wisp. You may like more smoke flavor than I do, just don't overdo it.

The brand of lump charcoal you use makes a difference. All natural hardwood charcoal is hard wood, but not the same hard wood. The denser the lump, the less smoke it gives off by itself, and the longer it will last with less ash. The softer the lump, which is usually less expensive, gives off more smoke and burns faster and leaves more ash. I prefer Ranch T or Wicked Good Charcoal because they are both harder. It takes more effort to light, but it is worth it. I will use any charcoal I can get if I have no choice, but I will monitor the fire more closely. The Naked Whiz has a charcoal "database" with ratings and reviews. Another advantage of hard lump is that it is less likely to have pieces and dust in the bag.

I also like hard lump because I can decide which wood chunks or chips I add to it to create the smoke. When I use chunks, I do not soak them or add too many. I usually use three for a long cook. I put them in the Egg when it comes up to my target temperature and let them smolder until the smoke dies down to a bluish-gray color, about 10 to 15 minutes. I don't use chunks for short cooks, nor do I use chips. I will let the minimal smoke from the lump do the smoke flavoring. It is your choice if you want to use chips. Soak them first for at least an hour and let the smoke settle down the same as if you were using chunks.

The type of wood chunks or chips also makes a difference. Hickory and mesquite can be very strong. Personally, I think mesquite is too strong. I use some hickory with big cuts of beef and pork, and pecan is a bit less smoky and is good for all big meats. Fruit woods like apple and peach go well with pork and poultry and are a little sweeter. Cherry and maple are similar and can also be used with beef. Cherry will add a little red color. A great source for wood chunks is Smokalicious.

How much smoke and what kind of charcoal, chunks or chips, is a personal preference. Just don't start out too strong, or you might have regrets. Cooking on the Egg with a little smoke is much better than using a conventional oven!

CLEANING THE EGG

At many of our demos, someone who is Eggcurious asks how to clean the Egg. The answer is rather simple and even easier to perform. The Egg is a self-cleaning oven. Get it up to 800°F (427°C) for 30 minutes and all the accumulated crud on the inside of the dome will turn to dust. After 30 minutes or so, close the bottom vent and put the rain cap on the top vent. Do NOT open the Egg. Let the Egg cool for at least one hour. Carefully burp the Egg and be wary of flashback. When the dome is cool enough for you to touch, wipe the inside with a soap-less plastic dish scrubber or sponge. You can spray a little water to help remove the dust, but it might be a little messier than doing it dry. There I go again, wet versus dry!

If it has been very humid and you haven't used your Egg in a while, mold may form on the grid or in the dome. Check to see if the charcoal is moldy, and if it is, discard it. To clean the mold, follow the same procedure as above.

Grates can be cleaned in the Egg, too, but the temperature doesn't have to be as hot: 400°F (200°C) to 500°F (260°C) will turn any baked-on food to petrified crust, which can be brushed off. I often switch my racks when doing indirect and put the dirtier one under the plate setter to clean while I do my cook.

Grease and moisture will make their way through the ceramic to the outside of the Egg because it is porous. This may be more obvious after a hot fire to clean the inside. You can clean the outside with a nonabrasive scrubbing sponge and water.

MOVING THE EGG AROUND AND TRANSPORT

When you buy an Egg from a dealer, you have the option to buy an accessory to set the Egg into or onto. The most common is the Egg "nest." I recommend the nest if you are not sure if you will have a table and you are going to keep your Egg mostly in one spot. The Egg sits into it, the nest, which has casters to allow careful maneuvering on hard surfaces. Big Green Egg also makes a "handler," which is a handle system attached to the bottom nest and the hinge assembly on the Egg. I recommend the handler if you don't think you will have a table and you plan to move the Egg around, say from the shed or garage to the backyard. This creates an easier way to roll the Egg around, but the Egg cannot come out of the nest without unbolting the handler. When using the nest with the handler, or just the nest alone, always drag the Egg toward you, never push it. The Egg is top heavy, and it doesn't take much to tip it over or tip it off balance. Your Egg is very precious. Pull it toward you, and if it tips and falls, at least it has a soft landing spot. I can't say much for your backside or ribs, but priorities have been set.

You can purchase tables to set your Egg into, which have counter and storage space. Big Green Egg also makes collapsible shelves to attach to the side of the bottom hinge band of the Egg. Some Eggheads prefer to build their Egg into their outdoor patio or make their own table. The Naked Whiz has a table picture gallery of over 200 homemade tables.

Transporting the Egg is not hard, but it requires a bit of planning. Most importantly, the Egg itself needs to be strapped down so it will not move when you go over a bump. If it is in a table in the back of a truck or trailer, tie both the Egg and the table down. If the Egg is in a nest, do the same thing. If you remove it from the table or nest for transport, make sure it is wrapped with padding under and around it to keep the porcelain from chipping or getting scratched. Big Green Egg also makes a carrier that attaches to a Class IV trailer hitch. If you need to, strap the Egg in the front seat with the air bag and ask your wife to sit in the backseat. Remember, priorities!

Lifting the Egg can be difficult. Two or more people are helpful. You can put two hands in the bottom vent, balancing the Egg and holding on to the hinge. It is best that you don't touch the hinge when lifting the Egg, because the band can slip off and send the dome flying. You can also take the dome off and remove the fire box and fire ring to make it lighter. I transport my Eggs all over with the fire box and fire ring, plate setter and grids inside and have never had a problem when they were strapped down.

If transporting the Egg is too cumbersome, or your wife wants the front seat back, you can buy a smaller Egg just for trips or leave an Egg at each place you frequently travel to. As I said earlier, every place I have a pillow, I have an Egg!

COVERS

I cover my Egg when it is outdoors. The rain and snow don't harm the ceramic, but some of the exposed metal parts may start to corrode over time. Also, a cover will keep pollen and bird crap off of your beautiful Egg. I prefer the black fabric premium cover from Big Green Egg. It is heavy and won't crack over time like plastic-coated covers will.

CARE FOR THE DUTCH OVEN, DAISY WHEEL AND WOK

Cast iron is very durable and will last for hundreds of years if taken care of properly. The Dutch oven and daisy wheel are both made of cast iron. Many new Dutch ovens are seasoned at purchase but may need to be re-seasoned. Wash cast iron only in hot water; never use soap. Use a plastic scraper or plastic scrubber to remove any burned on food. When clean, let dry thoroughly and wipe with a little vegetable oil. If the seasoning is worn, or there is any rust, scrub rust off with steel wool and wipe the whole oven inside and out with vegetable oil. Place upside down in a 350°F (180°C) oven or your Egg for one hour, with foil beneath to catch any oil drips. Let it cool completely in the oven and repeat two more times. Your daisy wheel can be seasoned the same way, by removing any rust and reseasoning in your oven.

A carbon steel wok needs to be seasoned as well. When it is new, it may have some oils on it to keep it from corroding. These need to be removed. Use hot, soapy water and a steel wool scouring pad to clean the inside and the outside. This will be the last time you use soap and steel wool in the wok. Dry completely and rub with vegetable oil inside and out. Bake in the oven for 20 minutes at 475°F (246°C). Let it completely cool in the oven and repeat twice more. If your wok has handles that could burn or melt in the oven, you will need to season it on the cook top: coat the inside with oil, heat for 5 minutes, cool and repeat twice.

Cast iron and steel woks are seasoned and you should not use steel utensils, which could scratch and damage the seasoning. Never scrub them with steel wool unless you are reseasoning them. The more you use a cast-iron or a carbon steel wok correctly, the more seasoned and nonstick it will become.

RESOURCES

ACCESSORIES

The Big Green Egg www.biggreenegg.com. The "Mothership," where you can find product description, information and a dealer locator

The Ceramic Grill Store www.ceramicgrillstore.com. Accessories and supplies that can be used on the Big Green Egg

A-Maze-N Products, LLC www. amazenproducts.com. Cold smoking accessories and flavored smoking pellets

Thermoworks www.thermoworks.com. Thermapen thermometer

Salt Rox www.saltrox.xom. Himalayan salt blocks for the Egg

RUBS AND SAUCES

Dizzy Pig BBQ Company www.dizzypigbbq.com. Rubs, instructional videos, recipes, Big Green Eggs and accessories

Moxie® www.drinkmoxie.com

The Slabs www.theslabs.com

Texas Pepper Jelly www.texaspepperjelly.com. Grilling and finishing sauces and the best fruit-flavored pepper jelly you will ever taste!

WOOD CHIPS AND CHUNKS

Smokinlicious www.smokinlicious.com

ORGANIZATIONS AND INFORMATION

Kansas City Barbecue Society (KCBS) www.kcbs.us

New England Barbecue Society (NEBS) www.nebs.org

Operation Barbecue Relief www.operationbbqrelief.org. OBR is a nonprofit volunteer disaster response group of families, individuals and barbecue teams who respond to natural disaster emergencies across the U.S., providing hot meals to those directly affected, emergency personnel and first responders. Get involved, whether providing financial assistance, your product or your time. It is a great cause!

The Big Green Egg forum www.eggheadforum.com

The Original Big Green Egg forum www.greeneggers.com

Big Green Egg BBQers Facebook Page

Naked Whiz www.nakedwhiz.com. Lump charcoal database and resources

ABOUT THE AUTHOR

 Eric lives in Bedford, New Hampshire. He is the author of *Smoke It Like a Pro* and has been cooking on the Big Green Egg since 2000. In 2006, Eric and his wife, Cindi, formed Yabba Dabba Que! Competition Barbecue Team and started competing at barbecue contests throughout the Northeast. In 2007, they were the New England Barbecue Society's (NEBS) rookie team of the year. In 2009 and 2012, Yabba Dabba Que! competed in the Jack Daniel's World Championships Invitational® in Lynchburg, Tennessee. In 2009, at the American Royal World Series of Barbecue®, the largest competition in the world, they received a perfect score for their crème brûlée entry!

Eric and Cindi are members of the Kansas City Barbecue Society (KCBS) and the New England Barbecue Society (NEBS). Eric was a three-term director of NEBS and its recording secretary. Eric has been a KCBS certified barbecue judge since 2006.

Eric and Cindi have attended and cooked at several Eggfests in Waldorf, Maryland; Brentwood, New Hampshire; and Manassas, Virginia. For the past seven years, they have been performing Big Green Egg demonstrations at dealerships.

ACKNOWLEDGMENTS

First, I would like to thank my wife, Cindi, for her love and support and for encouraging me to write this second book. Also for typing the manuscript, testing my recipes and putting up with me in all our barbecue escapades.

Special thanks to our friends Chuck and Nancy Helwig, Smokin' Aces Championship Barbecue Team; Don and Leslie Lovely, KCBS reps; and Jared and Suzanne Huizenga, Insane Swine Championship Barbecue Team for all your help and hard work with the photo shoot. We couldn't have done it without you.

Thank you to Will Kiester, Marissa Giambelluca, Meg Palmer and everyone at Page Street Publishing.

Thank you to Ken Goodman for his beautiful photography, which makes the recipes look as good as they taste!

INDEX